God finds us

Other Books by Jim Manney

A Simple, Life-Changing Prayer: Discovering the Power of St. Ignatius Loyola's Examen

What's Your Decision? How to Make Choices with Confidence and Clarity, with J. Michael Sparough and Tim Hipskind

Charged with Grandeur: The Book of Ignatian Inspiration
(editor)

God finds us

**An Experience of
the Spiritual Exercises of St. Ignatius Loyola**

JIM MANNEY

LOYOLA PRESS.
A JESUIT MINISTRY
Chicago

LOYOLA PRESS.
A JESUIT MINISTRY

3441 N. Ashland Avenue
Chicago, Illinois 60657
(800) 621-1008
www.loyolapress.com

Scripture quotations contained herein are from the New Revised Standard
Version Bible: Catholic Edition, copyright ©1993 and 1989 by the Division of
Christian Education of the National Council of the Churches of Christ in the
U.S.A. Used by permission. All rights reserved.

Unless otherwise noted, quotes from the Spiritual Exercises are from *The
Spiritual Exercises of St. Ignatius: Based on Studies in the Language of the Autograph*
by Louis J. Puhl, SJ (Chicago: Loyola Press, 1951).

Where indicated, material from the Spiritual Exercises is taken from
Understanding the Spiritual Exercises: A Handbook for Retreat Directors by Michael
Ivens, SJ (Herefordshire, U.K.: Gracewing, 1998). Used by permission.

Cover art credit: Joe Ginsberg/Stockbyte/Getty Images.

Library of Congress Cataloging-in-Publication Data
Manney, Jim.
  God finds us : an experience of the spiritual exercises of St. Ignatius Loyola /
Jim Manney.
      p. cm.
  Includes bibliographical references.
  ISBN-13: 978-0-8294-3827-7
  ISBN-10: 0-8294-3827-0
1. Ignatius, of Loyola, Saint, 1491-1556. Exercitia spiritualia.
2. Spirituality—Catholic Church. 3. Spiritual exercises. I. Title.
  BX2179.L8M326 2013
  248.3—dc23
                                                                    2012043285

Printed in the United States of America.
15 16 17 18 Versa 10 9 8 7 6 5 4 3 2

Contents

Preface   vii

Chapter 1   What Are the Spiritual
             Exercises?   1

Chapter 2   What Gets You out of Bed in
             the Morning?   15
             A Conversion of the Heart

Chapter 3   Presuppositions and Prayers   27
             Before the Exercises Begin

Chapter 4   It's Not about You   39
             The First Principle and Foundation

Chapter 5   Loved Sinners   49
             The Mystery of Sin

Chapter 6   There's Work to Be Done   65
             The Call of the King

Chapter 7   "You're Gonna Have to Serve
             Somebody"   79
             The Two Standards

Chapter 8   Free at Last?   93
             The Three Classes of People

Chapter 9   "It's Supposed to Be Hard"   105
             The Three Kinds of Humility

Chapter 10   What Are You Feeling?   121
             Discerning the Spirits

Chapter 11   It Seemed Like a Good Idea at
             the Time   137
             Making Decisions

Chapter 12   "Take This Soul
             and Make It Sing"   153
             Finding God in All Things

Epilogue   165
             Limping to the Finish Line

Further Reading and Notes on Sources   169

Acknowledgments   177

About the Author   178

Preface

A few years ago, I made the Spiritual Exercises of St. Ignatius Loyola with the help of a cheerful Jesuit named Dennis. I had always thought of the Exercises as the spiritual equivalent of Navy SEAL training or hiking the Appalachian Trail—something for highly trained, disciplined, ambitious people who aren't satisfied with anything short of the toughest challenge. I'm not one of those people. I'm a baseball fan in the Midwest with a mortgage, a family, two cars, and a full-time job. I'm a pretty ordinary guy, but I made the Exercises anyway, and they did me a lot of good. If I can make the Spiritual Exercises, just about anybody can. That's one reason I wrote this book—to plant the idea in your mind that the Spiritual Exercises might be helpful for you, too.

The Exercises don't feature theology, doctrine, devotional practices, or other "churchy" stuff. Ignatius assumes a Christian outlook; he was a European Catholic writing in the sixteenth century, after all. But Ignatius was more interested in what you feel than what you think. His Exercises aim for a changed heart more than a changed mind—although it's certainly true that you'll think about things differently as a result of making the Exercises. He built the Exercises around certain experiences that led him to the ideas and themes that he thought would bring about a "conversion of the heart." These themes are my gateway into the Exercises. I've built this book around them. By explaining them, I hope to give a sense of what the Exercises are about.

I'm not going to discuss everything that's in the Exercises with the same degree of detail. I'll concentrate on the major themes; I won't cover everything. Still, I hope that reading this book will give you a sense of what making the Exercises is like. Maybe it can be a kind of retreat for you. To that end, I've drawn on my own experiences of the Exercises, and I talk about the themes in roughly the order that you'd take them up if you were doing the Exercises yourself.

I hope you do that. I'm an unabashed fan of the Spiritual Exercises. I think they are very "modern." They fit the temper of our times well. But they don't fit the times perfectly;

if they did, they wouldn't be worth the trouble. In fact, they appeal especially to people who don't feel completely at home in the world as it is, people who aren't satisfied with the conventional wisdom, people who are looking for something different. If that's you, read on.

Chapter 1

What Are the Spiritual Exercises?

What *are* the Spiritual Exercises? The question isn't as easy to answer as you might think. Two different things are called "the Spiritual Exercises." One is a book, *The Spiritual Exercises*, which you can hold in your hands and read. These days you can also read it on your Kindle or listen to it on your MP3 player. The book is a guide for the other "Spiritual Exercises"—a prayer-retreat experience. That experience is my main focus in the pages to come. But let's look at the book first.

The Spiritual Exercises was written in spare, dense language in the sixteenth century by St. Ignatius Loyola, a remarkable spiritual innovator and one of the true giants of Christian history. I first picked up the book when I was in college, but I didn't get very far. No wonder: Ignatius didn't write the book for people like me who were looking for some good spiritual reading. He wrote it for the spiritual directors who guide people on this retreat. In fact, Ignatius didn't want people who are making the Exercises to read too much of the book. It's just as well. To be frank, the book is a hard slog. Ignatius was a man of immense and manifold talents, but a felicitous prose style wasn't one of them. You might say of *The Spiritual Exercises* what Mark Twain said of one of the novels of Henry James: "Once you put it down, it's hard to pick it up again."

The book originated in Ignatius's personal experiences in prayer over an eleven-month period in the town of Manresa in northeastern Spain. He developed the book over a period of about twenty years, revising and editing as his spiritual life deepened and as he gained experience in helping others have the same life-changing experience he had had. The book contains exercises, reflections, prayers, scenarios, Scripture readings, and other material for an intensive personal encounter with Jesus. This encounter is the other "Spiritual Exercises"—the prayer-retreat experience that is my main focus. This experience is a bit hard to describe because everyone's experience is uniquely his or her own, but here's my stab at a definition: The Spiritual Exercises is a structured program of prayer, reflection, and self-scrutiny, usually done with the help of a spiritual director, with the goal of allowing God to free us to love and to serve in the concrete circumstances of our lives.

For a long time (I'm talking centuries here), someone like me would never have gotten near the Spiritual Exercises. They *were* the spiritual equivalent of Navy SEAL training—a grueling, intense thirty-day retreat in a rural retreat house, experienced in silence, cut off from the outside world. The people who made the Exercises were mainly clergy and religious, those considering a religious vocation, and those laypeople with the desire and wherewithal to get away for thirty days. But Ignatius envisioned other ways to make the Exercises. He was still a layman when he developed them, and the first people to make the Exercises were also laypeople. Ignatius told spiritual directors to be creative in adapting the Exercises to people's circumstances.

In recent years, spiritual directors have done just that. New forms of the Exercises have been developed, and more people have been making them than ever before. People make the Exercises for many reasons. Many are making big decisions—about marriage, career, religious vocation, and the like. Many have a restless feeling that they're ready for something new; perhaps the kids have moved out, or retirement is drawing near—they sense that a new chapter in their life is about to begin. Many people make the Exercises simply because they want to experience more of God. That's why I decided to do them.

The most common way to make the Exercises nowadays is in the form of a "retreat in daily life." There are other ways to make the Exercises: eight-day retreats, group retreats, and self-guided retreats. You'll even find several versions of an Ignatian retreat on the Web. And, of course, you can always make the traditional thirty-day retreat in a retreat house if you're up for it.

A Retreat at Home

When people ask me what the Spiritual Exercises are like, I usually describe what they were like for me. My experience is my own, of course, but I think that the way I made the Exercises is fairly typical of the way most people do them today. I did a "retreat in daily life." For about seven months, I spent some time every day praying and reflecting on the day's exercises, and I met with my spiritual director Dennis once a week to discuss what I was experiencing. All the while, I worked at my job, did chores around the house, traveled a bit for work and family visits, watched some football on TV, and generally lived a normal life.

When I started thinking seriously about making the Spiritual Exercises, I was afraid of getting in over my head. I'm a little embarrassed to say why. It wasn't so much the Exercises' daunting reputation, or their length, or a fear that they would take me to a place I didn't want to go. I was worried about the commitment to pray every day for a substantial period of time. I've never been a great pray-er. I was afraid of getting distracted and bored, and then feeling guilty when I couldn't keep the commitment. But it wasn't as hard as I thought it would be. I had plenty to do. I didn't get bored at all; in fact, some days I had to stop before I wanted to.

This is how it went.

Every morning I would go to a quiet place for about forty-five minutes, sometimes longer. When I was out of town, this place was a hotel room or a guest bedroom, but most of the time it was the spare downstairs bedroom in my home. To find the time, I made some sacrifices; I got up a little earlier than usual, and I didn't sleep as much as I wanted to on weekends. These changes seemed like a big deal before I made them, but they weren't. They were changes in my routine, and soon they became the new routine.

In my prayer place, I would go through a few settling-down rituals and briefly review what happened in the previous day. Then I would pick up a sheet Dennis had given me with that week's exercises. Each day's exercise begins with a prayer for a specific grace; Ignatius believed that we should ask God for what we want—explicitly and directly. Sometimes this was easy, as when the grace was "to know Jesus more intimately, to love him more intensely, and to follow him more closely." Sometimes it was hard to ask for it; the grace for one section of the Exercises is "a healthy sense of shame and confusion before God as I consider the effects of sin in my life, my community, and my world." When I couldn't honestly say that I wanted that day's grace, I would pray to *want* to want it.

Then I would turn to the day's meditation, assigned by Dennis. These meditations are the "exercises" in the Spiritual Exercises. Most of these are passages from the Bible: Gospel scenes, psalms, readings from the Hebrew prophets, and readings from Paul's letters, most of which have to do with the life and meaning of Jesus. Some were meditations that Ignatius wrote—"what if" thought experiments designed to make a point or draw out a response. I'd read the material several times and ask the Holy Spirit to help me engage it in two ways: with my mind for understanding and with my heart for feeling. I made good use of a couple of prayer techniques Ignatius developed to help people engage the exercises with feeling.

Then I would pick up a pen and write about what I sensed God doing in the morning's prayer. Everything would go in my journal: insights, questions, doubts, feelings, impressions, "senses," and notes. Every week I'd take these notes and discuss them with Dennis. He'd make comments, point out things I hadn't noticed, and make suggestions. Dennis loves poetry, contemporary fiction, movies, and Broadway shows, so these made their way into our discussions. Once he suggested that I read the novel *Henderson the Rain King* by Saul Bellow. Henderson is a man plagued by a spiritual void and driven by an inner voice crying, "I want, I want." His ailment is one that Ignatius diagnoses very well in the Spiritual Exercises. Another time Dennis suggested I watch the Stephen Sondheim musical *Into the Woods*; he even lent me the DVD. The characters in the play cut corners and behave badly in pursuit of their dreams, and they suffer the consequences. They learn the difference between superficial wants and what they *really* want. (I don't want to give the impression that making the Exercises is an excursion into literature and pop culture. Dennis also gave me plenty of more traditional spiritual reading.)

Read, pray, reflect, write—that's how it went, day after day. I'd talk to Dennis every week and receive a new sheet of exercises. I'd pray and reflect in the mornings, and read the other material Dennis had suggested when I had the time. I'd keep track of the feelings that all this material stirred in me. I tried to listen to what my "heart" was saying. Gradually, I became more sensitive to where God was in my everyday life. Gradually I understood that God is at work in my world and in my life, and that my task is to respond to the invitation God is offering.

The fundamental experience was one of coming to know Jesus. Most of the daily exercises are Scripture passages from the Gospels. By entering those stories, I walked with Jesus through his public ministry, passion, death, and resurrection. Everything in the Exercises happens within the context of coming to know Jesus more intimately and loving him more deeply. This is probably the biggest difference the Spiritual Exercises made in my life. In one of her novels, Flannery O'Connor says of a character that Jesus was "a ragged figure flitting from tree to tree at the back of his mind." Jesus had been something like that for me. When the Exercises were over, though, Jesus had come up front.

Another difference had to do with the way I look at the emotional side of life. I'm a "feeler"; the Myers-Briggs Type

Indicator personality test says so. But I also live in my head a lot, especially in matters of faith and religion, ironically enough. The Spiritual Exercises opened a vista of other ways of "knowing"—feelings, intuitions, awarenesses, and other non-cognitive routes to understanding.

What the Daydreaming Soldier Noticed

Many people who've made the Spiritual Exercises have had an experience similar to mine. That's no accident; this is what Ignatius wanted the Spiritual Exercises to do. He knew what he was after because he knew what he wanted and he had experienced it himself. So to answer the question "What are the Spiritual Exercises?" you have to get to know Ignatius.

Ignatius was a bona fide intellectual, a graduate of the University of Paris, but before studying at one of the best universities in the world at the time, he was a soldier and courtier in the service of the kingdom of Castile. His macho world came tumbling down in 1521, when he was wounded in a battle against the French at the city of Pamplona, and then carted back to his family's castle in northern Spain to recuperate. If you've spent any time with Jesuits, you've probably heard the story of Ignatius's conversion. If you've spent a *lot* of time with Jesuits, you've heard the story many times. It's the "Genesis story" of Ignatian spirituality. Buddhism was born when the prince Siddhartha ventured beyond his palace and encountered human suffering. Franciscans trace their spirituality to the day St. Francis of Assisi kissed a leper. Ignatian spirituality started at the sickbed of a wounded, vain, bored ex-soldier.

Ignatius had fallen very low. He had been an ambitious "man on the make" at court, loved by the ladies, admired by his friends, and feared by his enemies. (Once he was arrested for brawling in the street, making him one of the few saints with a police record.) But all in all, it was a pretty empty life. I suspect he knew it was empty. He was a very smart man, and it didn't take a genius to see that the medieval tradition of chivalry and knightly valor was fading in the first decades of the sixteenth century. In any case, he was then a thirty-year-old, washed-up knight with two bad legs, living at home, being nursed back to health by his sister-in-law. He was ready for something new.

Ignatius possessed several gifts. He was a talented daydreamer with an active imagination. He had a lot of time on his hands, and he dreamed about glory in battle and amorous conquests—the life he had lived, and the life he might still be living if the cannonball had taken a slightly different path and missed his legs. Ignatius also dreamed about the stories he read in the only two books in the house—one on the life of Christ and the other on the lives of the saints. He imagined what it would be like to be a knight in the service of Christ. The stories of St. Francis and St. Dominic fired his imagination. They were great saints, but Ignatius thought he could be an even *greater* saint than they were, given the chance and the inclination. As I said—Ignatius was a dreamer.

Ignatius had another talent: he was a keen observer of people and of himself. We might call him a self-aware postmodernist working at the dawn of modernity. Ignatius observed himself daydreaming, and what he noticed was this: dreams of romance and military glory left him depressed; dreams of following Christ left him excited and inspired. He realized that his surface feelings of angst and discontent, and of joy and delight, were pointing to deeper things. It dawned on him that God was speaking to him through his feelings. His feelings were indicating which possible future would give him lasting joy and which wouldn't. The sadness that came upon him after he dreamed about his former life meant that a life at court would bring him no satisfaction. His excitement after dreaming about following Christ meant that that was the direction that would fulfill his deepest desires. Eventually, he decided to follow the direction his feelings indicated. To the dismay of his family and friends, he put on the clothes of a poor man and hit the road to go wherever God might lead him.

This Is How the Spiritual Exercises Came to Be

Early on, Ignatius decided that his mission was to help people to love and serve God, so he began to apply what he learned about desires and feelings to his efforts to help his friends find their way in life. He made friends easily. He was the kind of man you'd notice when he showed up in your town. You'd want to be around him. Once you got to know him, he'd be the guy you'd go to if you needed some advice, and you'd probably do your best to follow his suggestions. So Ignatius made suggestions, observed their effect, and made notes about what helped and what didn't. These notes grew into *The Spiritual Exercises.* He had a talent for organizing material for maximum impact. He'd be the perfect patron saint for editors and theater producers and PowerPoint presenters.

I'm not a big fan of spiritual systems and theories. So it pleased me to discover that the Spiritual Exercises aren't mere theory; they emerged from Ignatius's experience and the experience of hundreds of people who worked with him.

Ignatius did not think up a system. He discovered things that are true about the way God and human beings interact, and he put these insights into the form of a retreat suitable for virtually anyone with a generous spirit and an open mind.

It's not a one-size-fits-all scheme for renewal. It's not a recipe. It's not a cookbook. It's not a course. It's an invitation to discover what will truly make you happy. It's an invitation to fall in love.

Chapter 2

What Gets You out of Bed in the Morning?

A Conversion of the Heart

I have a friend who grew up in a secular home and knew nothing about Christianity until she was an adult. While in her thirties, she embarked on a spiritual quest and began by studying Christianity. She read catechisms and creeds and theology and came away very impressed. She told me, "Whoever thought up this Christian stuff really knew what he was doing." I had the same sort of feeling about the Spiritual Exercises: whoever thought this up really knew what he was doing. My father was an engineer; he liked to look under the hood of cars to see how they worked. I'm a professional editor; I like to look under the hood of books to see how they work. The Spiritual Exercises work very well.

A lot of thought went into them. The parts fit together. Ignatius, the man who put it all together, had something definite in mind.

What Are You in Love With?

What exactly *did* Ignatius have in mind? Many experts say that the Exercises are about helping us make good decisions. That's surely true: early in the Exercises we ask, "What have I done for Christ? What am I doing for Christ? What ought I to do for Christ?" These questions loom over the whole experience of the Exercises; you keep coming back to them. The Exercises have a lot to say about discernment, and one important section is devoted to making a major life decision, if one is in the offing. But the Exercises are about other things too. They are about prayer—they've been called "a school of prayer." They are about repentance and forgiveness. They are about knowing more about yourself. They are about generosity of spirit. Above all, they are about encountering Jesus.

Something Pedro Arrupe said sums up what Ignatius had in mind. Arrupe was superior general of the Jesuits from 1965 to 1983. By all accounts, he was a lovable, enchanting man, deeply spiritual and infectiously optimistic. I think of him as one of those rare characters who lights up the room, who makes you feel like he's your best friend as soon as you shake his hand. A personality something like Ignatius's, I think. A saying attributed to Arrupe begins: "Nothing is more practical than finding God, that is, than falling in love in a quite absolute, final way." It's what Arrupe said next that strikes me.

> What you are in love with, what seizes your imagination, will affect everything. It will decide what will get you out of bed in the morning, what you will do with your evenings, how you will spend your weekends, what you read, who you know, what breaks your heart, and what amazes you with joy and gratitude. Fall in love, stay in love and it will decide everything.

I don't know a better description of what Ignatius of Loyola intended when he put the Spiritual Exercises together. He wants us to fall in love. He's interested in those deep currents of feeling that shape what we want, which in turn influences what we do. Psychologists talk about the three parts of the mind: the cognitive (reason and other mental processes), the conative (the will), and the affective (feelings and emotions). Ignatius zeroed in on the "affect." Understanding is important, and the will is vital, but what gets you out of bed in the morning is what you love. This is what Ignatius wanted the Spiritual Exercises to influence.

Exercises for the Spirit

Ignatius set out to influence what we love with a program of spiritual exercises that he described as "ways of examining one's conscience, of meditating, contemplating, of praying vocally and mentally." He compared them to physical exercises: "strolling, walking, running." The Spiritual Exercises have a schedule, an order, and a goal. You might think of the Exercises as a training program designed to bring about a high degree of spiritual fitness—the spiritual equivalent of getting your body into shape. When you're in training you work, you do new things, you stretch yourself, you follow instructions, and you trust the process. You listen to the coach and do what the coach says.

To help people engage this material *affectively*—with the heart more than with the mind—Ignatius developed several unique methods of praying. One is imaginative prayer. He has us place ourselves as a participant inside a scene described in a Scripture passage or a meditation, employing all the senses to *feel* what's going on, as if we were really there. Another method of Ignatian prayer is the "colloquy"—a conversation between the person and

God. Colloquies are honest, intimate, personal conversations between friends. Another prayer method—the most important—is the daily examen, a way of reviewing the day that pays particular attention to where God has been present.

Ignatius arranged his material in four major sections called "weeks." During the first week, we do a thorough stocktaking of our lives. We look at where we stand with God, with others, and with ourselves, making an honest assessment of the ways we have fallen short. The other three weeks are focused on deepening a relationship with Jesus and reflecting on the implications of Jesus' invitation to work with him in healing the world. In the second week, we follow Jesus through his public ministry. In the third week, we follow him through his last supper, agony in the garden, arrest and trial, passion, and death. In the fourth week, we meet the resurrected Jesus and celebrate his continuing presence in our world and in our lives.

A Story That Feels True

This is the Christian story, but the arc of it—surrender, suffering, death, and rebirth—is an archetypal human story that's planted deep in our psyches. It *feels* true. The ancient Greeks and Romans told this story. So did Shakespeare and

Muhammad, the Buddha and Tolstoy. Week 1: the human condition—everyone suffers, everyone fails, and everyone is powerless to change anything fundamental about it. Week 2: change is possible—if we surrender our illusions of mastery and turn ourselves over to God. Week 3: redemption beckons, but first comes struggle. We suffer, but God is with us. Week 4: out of the crucible of suffering come love and redemption.

Christians (theologians, anyway) call this story the paschal mystery—the passion, death, and resurrection of Jesus, which Jesus' followers live out again and again throughout their lives. Buddhists might call this pattern the struggle to achieve enlightenment. Muslims understand it as repeated acts of surrender to God. For Jews, it's the story of their people. In college, I had a smart-aleck friend who didn't think Christianity was true because versions of the story of the suffering, dying, and rising God are found in the myths of many cultures. I think that's an argument for the *truth* of Christianity. Every human heart is prepared to hear the story of Jesus because it fits—it fits our reality and rings true to our experience.

Let's look at what Ignatius says about the purpose of the Exercises. He writes that they're for "making ourselves ready to get rid of disordered affections so that, once rid of them, one might seek and find the divine will in regard to the disposition of one's life." Ignatius chose his words carefully, so let's take that sentence apart.

"Making ourselves ready"

The idea in the first phrase is key: we make ourselves ready. We don't make things happen in the Exercises; God does. The Spiritual Exercises are a matter of *preparing for something to happen.* This challenged me right off the bat. My default attitude (and I don't think I'm alone in this) is that *I* make things happen. If I put in the effort, God will reward me. Not so. Whatever happens in the Exercises is God's doing and originates in God's love for us. But "making ourselves ready" in the Exercises isn't a passive waiting around. It involves work, lots of it. But all this work is designed to put us in the place where God can give us what we need, or to put it a better way, to make us able to *receive* what God has been giving us all along.

You've probably heard this before; it's hardly a novel insight to say that we receive what God gives. A friend of mine says that the basis of all true religion is summed up in the phrase "there is a God—and I'm not him." But the temptation to think we're in charge is always there, so it's no wonder that Ignatius reminds us right at the start that the work we do in the Spiritual Exercises is laying the ground-work for God to do something. The Spiritual Exercises is not an exercise in self-help personal improvement. We're not in charge here.

"To get rid of disordered affections"

What we do in the Exercises is *get rid of disordered affections*. We'll come back to this idea again and again. "Disordered affections" sounds faintly musty, like a phrase from a Victorian novel: "When she spied Mr. Darcy arriving in his carriage, Elizabeth was stricken with a storm of disordered affections." Or a bit pedantic, like a term from the *Diagnostic and Statistical Manual of Mental Disorders*: "disordered affections is an indicator of a narcissistic personality." But disordered affections are a key idea of the Spiritual Exercises. Buddhists strive to extinguish desire. Existentialists defy the void by creating meaning through free choices. Followers of Ignatius seek to become free of disordered affections.

Ignatius isn't talking about "affections" as we popularly understand them: a fondness for your nieces and nephews or a liking for rich desserts. He means the things that drive you, that you're in love with, that get you out of bed in the morning (or keep you there). His disordered affections are more like an obsessive craving for chocolate cake when you're on a diet. A desire to make a lot of money might be a disordered affection. So might a yearning for the limelight, a hunger to give the orders instead of following them, or a longing to be admired. Physical fitness, knowledge, sexual pleasure, high social status—the list of affections is long, and all of them can become disordered. These are the desires that control what we do.

The only affection we can afford to totally indulge in is love of God and neighbor. All the others can become disordered. There's nothing wrong with making money. But there's probably a lot wrong with it if you uproot your family five times in eight years and work ninety-hour weeks to make the money you think you need. It's terrific when others praise you for a job well done. It's not so terrific when you crave attention and become jealous of the good fortune of others. Sex is one of the great joys in life. Sex with the wrong person can be a calamity. The affections we need to get rid of are *disordered* affections—literally, affections that are out of order. They are in the wrong place in our hierarchy of values.

Discerning when affections get disordered is hard. Getting rid of them is harder. We might have an idea of the things that drive us, but we're inclined not to look too closely. Usually, our motives are mixed. The motives for any important decision typically include the practical and the idealistic, the selfish and the generous, the fearful and the trusting, the realistic and the fanciful. Do you have too little ambition or too much? Are you too passive or too aggressive? What's "enough" money? These are hard questions to answer. The Exercises help you come to grips with them.

"So that one might seek and find the divine will"

The point of it all is to find out what God wants of us—"*to seek and find the divine will.*" We get rid of disordered affections because they confuse, obfuscate, and distort our idea of where true happiness lies. What does *God* want?

"God's will" is a slippery phrase. Years ago I met some young evangelicals who were hot on "the four spiritual laws." The first law was "God loves you and has a wonderful plan for your life." I liked the "God loves you" part, but I wasn't so keen on the plan for my life. I took this to mean a detailed "plan" tailored just for me: the woman I would marry, the work I would do, where I would live, the kind of car I would drive, and so on. I didn't really believe that God had plans like that; at least I hoped he didn't. I wanted to make my own decisions.

Ignatius recognized that God's will is not a precise blue-print, but neither is it a vague "whatever you want" blank check. God has a "plan" in the sense that he has an idea of the kind of person you can be and an idea of the life that would bring you the most joy. The broad outlines of God's idea are the same for everyone—to love and serve God and neighbor. But the particulars are unique to each of us. Finding God's will means discovering God's unique love for us, his desire to help us grow into our most authentic selves, and the way we can best serve him and his people. That's why we get rid of disordered affections. It's like a cook peeling an artichoke to get to the heart, or a sculptor chipping away at marble to find the beautiful form inside. Beneath the love of money, possessions, honor, and pride, we will find what we *really* want. And here is Ignatius's great insight. When we find what we really want, we find what God wants, too. It's a pretty remarkable idea, so I'll say it again: *when we discover what we really want, we discover what God wants, too.*

This insight has its roots in Ignatius's own experience on his sickbed. By reflecting on his feelings and daydreams, he realized that he would be happiest and most satisfied if he totally devoted himself to Christ. You might say, that's obvi-ous. God wants people to follow him. Christian daydreams are better than frivolous worldly ones, so it's no wonder they made Ignatius happy. But it's not so simple. Ignatius found the way of life best suited for *him*. If he had been a different person, it's entirely possible that a career of service to the Castilian king would have given him more happiness than a life as a priest. In fact, working for the king must have been God's desire for any number of young men in sixteenth-century Spain. But such a life wasn't his desire for Ignatius.

Ignatius didn't set out to discern "God's will." He discovered God's desire for him by discovering what his deepest desire was for himself. What he wanted and what God wanted were the same thing, and the way he discovered what he wanted was to pay close attention to his feelings. He came in through the back door—by noticing interior, affective experiences that led him to a new way of life. So it is with all of us. The promise of the Spiritual Exercises is that they can lead you to the way of life best suited for *you*. God's will isn't something external. It's internal. It's implanted in your heart.

Chapter 3

Presuppositions and Prayers

Before the Exercises Begin

Sometimes, Ignatius attracted the wrong kind of attention. In his midthirties, he set out to get a university degree because church authorities told him he couldn't teach others about spiritual matters without one. He started in Barcelona by learning Latin (in a class with young boys), enrolled at the University of Alcalá near Madrid, then moved on to the University of Salamanca. He made friends and talked a lot, and pretty soon word spread that this Basque ex-soldier who walked with a limp had some novel ideas. The religious authorities decided to check him out. One day the Dominicans on the theological faculty invited him over for dinner and a theological chat. They asked him whether his teaching was based on his learning or on the inspiration of the Holy Spirit. It was a trick question.

He couldn't claim to be learned because he didn't have the degree that would authorize him to teach; that's why he was in school. If he said he was inspired by the Holy Spirit, the authorities would suspect he was one of the Illuminati, a heretical sect whose members claimed to receive direct inspiration from God. It's not known exactly how Ignatius replied, but the Dominicans didn't like what they heard. They locked him up for several weeks until an official tribunal ruled that no error could be found in his teaching. Soon Ignatius left Spain for a more hospitable intellectual atmosphere in Paris. (Those Jesuit jokes that hinge on the rivalry between Jesuits and Dominicans have some basis in historical fact.)

The inquisitors might have been made nervous by Ignatius's view that each of us can have a unique personal relationship with God. This idea is central to the Spiritual Exercises. Ignatius puts it this way in an instruction to spiritual directors: "The director of the Exercises, . . . without leaning to one side or the other, should permit the Creator to deal directly with the creature, and the creature directly with his Creator and Lord." In other words, directors don't direct. They watch, listen, and make suggestions. They help create the environment where God can act. They don't stand between God and us. No one does. The Holy Spirit is the director of the Spiritual Exercises.

This is one of several important comments Ignatius makes before the Exercises begin. One that's especially significant is something he calls the "Presupposition." It's a ground rule. Before a baseball game, the managers and umpires go over the ground rules that determine whether a ball is fair or foul in the particular park they are playing in. The Presupposition is a ground rule laying out what's fair and what's foul in the Spiritual Exercises:

> To assure better cooperation between the one who is giving the Exercises and [the one making them], and more beneficial results for both, it is necessary to suppose that every good Christian is more ready to put a good interpretation on another's statement than to condemn it as false. If an orthodox construction cannot be put on a proposition, the one who made it should be asked how he understands it. If he is in error, he should be corrected with all kindness. If this does not suffice, all appropriate means should be used to bring him to a correct interpretation, and so defend the proposition from error.

Ignatius laid down this rule because in the sixteenth century the ecclesiastical air was full of accusations of heresy and bad faith. (Sound familiar?) He didn't want people to approach the Exercises with an attitude of suspicion, so he made it a rule that everyone had to put the best possible spin on one another's views. Ignatius is saying, "You're going to be hearing some new ideas that might bother you. When you do, assume the best, not the worst." Imagine what politics would be like if everyone were "more ready to put a good interpretation on another's statement than to condemn it as false." It's a good rule for communication between husbands and wives, for discussions between parents and children, and for business meetings of all kinds.

The Exercises are full of wisdom like this. These are some of my favorites: That people learn best when they discover things for themselves and not just do what they're told; that love is best expressed in deeds rather than words; that a good way to deal with temptation is to do the opposite; that the best use of material things is to further the goal for which one was created; that "relish" of the truth is more satisfying than mere knowledge of it.

The School of Ignatian Prayer

One presupposition is that the person making the Exercises should be able to pray in certain ways suited to the Exercises' heart-centered spirituality. It's no wonder that the Exercises have been called "a school of prayer." Ignatian prayer is a topic unto itself, but I'll say a few things about it here, because praying the Ignatian way is vital to making the Exercises well. It's also something that can make a big difference for you long after the Exercises are over.

Ignatian prayer cultivates a conscious, intimate, personal relationship with God. It's a relationship of friends. "You are my friends," Jesus said. "No one has greater love than this, to lay down one's life for his friends." The Jesuit William Barry says that "God desires humans into existence for the sake of friendship." Barry makes it a point to draw out the contrast between this friendship and conventional images of God. God our friend is not God the majestic, all-powerful, and distant ruler. The image is not God as lawgiver and judge. I'm a baseball fan, and I used to think about God as something like the manager of a baseball team who gets along well with his players—supportive, but also watchful and critical, ready to put me on the bench if I strike out too much. Remember that these are only analogies; anything we say about God is a mere shadow of the reality. But images do matter, and there's no question that "friend" describes the God we meet in the Exercises better than "scorekeeper" or "judge." As Father Barry's Irish mother put it, "God is better than he's made out to be."

In the Exercises, Ignatius wants us to engage every faculty we possess in a relationship with the almighty God who seeks our friendship. He invites us to prayer that uses our memory, understanding, will, imagination, judgment, and senses. Ignatius even cares about the physical part of prayer—when we stand, when we kneel, when we sit. All of this is designed in the Exercises to bring us into intimate contact with God.

The Examen: The Essential Prayer

The most important Ignatian prayer is the examen, a method of prayerfully reviewing your daily experience to detect God's presence and discern God's direction. I learned to pray the examen long before I made the Spiritual Exercises, and to say that this prayer made a big difference for me is an understatement. I even wrote a book about the examen—*A Simple, Life-Changing Prayer*. If you want to learn more about the examen, take a look at that book.

The examen prayer has five steps, which most people take more or less in order:

1. Give thanks—Begin in a spirit of gratitude. Everything is a gift from God.

2. Pray for light—Ask God for the grace to pray, to see, and to understand.

3. Review the day—Guided by the Holy Spirit, look back on your day. Pay attention to your experience. Look for God in it.

4. Look at what's wrong—Face up to failures and short-comings and weaknesses and challenges. Ask forgiveness for your faults. Ask God to show you how to improve.

5. Resolution for the day to come—What will you do in the day to come? Where do you need God today?

Ignatius teaches the examen at the very beginning of the Exercises, just before the Exercises proper begin. He regarded it as an essential tool for doing the Exercises. The examen assumes that Christ shows himself in *this* world, at *this* time, in our concrete circumstances; this is one of the recurring themes of the Exercises as a whole. The Exercises are about meeting Christ as the person you really are in the life you are actually living. The examen takes our personal experience seriously. If God is present in our world, then God is certainly present in our daily experience of the world. Our experience can be misleading, and we must carefully test the spiritual leadings that arise from it, but fundamentally, we can *trust* our experience. We can find God in the comings and goings of our daily lives.

The examen looks simple, but looks are deceiving. Ignatius thought it was *the* essential prayer. The only rule he made about prayer for the Jesuits was a requirement that they pray the examen twice a day—at noon and before sleep. A Jesuit can be working eighteen-hour days, too busy to pray normally, but he will still take some time to reflect on his daily experience to find out what God thinks about it. The examen is actually an attitude more than a prayer technique. It takes about fifteen or twenty minutes to review your day using the five steps of the examen, but this is only a start. The real purpose of the examen—and of the Spiritual Exercises—is to make us sensitive to the presence and action of God at *all* times, not just during special moments of prayer. Much of the Exercises involve precisely this kind of prayer. We strive for a reflective self-awareness: "Why am I attached to these things? What do I *really* want?"

Let Your Imagination Go

Years ago, my wife and I made a pilgrimage to the Holy Land. I had an aha moment riding on a bus in Galilee at the very beginning of the pilgrimage. The bus came over the crest of a hill, and the Sea of Galilee suddenly appeared before me, a blue jewel a few miles away. I was dumbstruck. Here was the Sea of Galilee—a real lake, not just a place in a story in a sacred book. It looked like lakes in northern Michigan where I'd gone fishing. Jesus had been *here*, seeing what I was seeing. I spent the whole pilgrimage in a kind of happy trance, fascinated by the idea that the Gospel stories I'd been hearing all my life had happened *here*, in this place.

Much of the prayer in the Spiritual Exercises aims for something like the experience I had on the pilgrimage. It's imaginative prayer, prayer that engages our imagination and senses to bring the Gospels to life. Ignatius will have you place yourself fully into a Gospel story. In a typical exercise, you'll be an onlooker at the side of the road, watching Jesus speaking to a blind man. You hear the man plead for healing. You note the disciples' irritation and the crowd's curiosity. The man beside you in the crowd jostles you as he strains to get a better view. You feel the hot sun, smell the dust. Above all, you watch Jesus—his gestures, the look in his eyes, the expression on his face, the way he walks. You hear him speak the words that are recorded in the Gospel. You go on to imagine other words he might have spoken and other deeds he might have done.

Ignatius proposes many scenes like this for imaginative contemplation. He tends to choose scenes of Jesus acting rather than ones of him teaching or telling parables. He wants us to see Jesus interacting with others, making decisions, moving about, ministering. He doesn't want us to *think* about Jesus. He wants us to *experience* him. He wants Jesus to fill our senses. He wants us to meet him. Praying this way day after day brings Jesus into places that the intellect does not touch. People I know who've had deep spiritual experiences often say, "Scripture came alive for me." Now I know what they mean.

To get the most out of imaginative prayer, you need to imagine what *isn't* written in the Gospels. What was it like in Lazarus's household on the evening of the day Jesus raised him from the dead? What did the disciples say to one another after the rich young man turned down Jesus' invitation to follow him? What would *you* have said if Jesus asked you, "Who do you say that I am?" Don't be afraid to let yourself go. The Holy Spirit is guiding your prayer.

An Intimate Conversation

Many times in the Exercises, Ignatius directs us to a form of prayer called a "colloquy." *Colloquy* is a fancy word for an intimate conversation. Jesus is our usual partner for these conversations, but occasionally Ignatius calls for colloquies with God the Father and Mary the mother of Jesus. Colloquies often occur at the end of a prayer period to emphasize the subject of the prayer, but this conversational prayer can take place at any time.

A colloquy is supposed to be a natural, free-flowing conversation. We speak and listen as the Spirit moves us, expressing ourselves as a friend speaks to a friend, or as a person speaks to one whom he or she has offended, or as a child speaks to a parent or mentor, or as a lover speaks to his or her beloved. Whatever the context, the colloquy requires us to be *real*, to speak from the heart. As in any meaningful conversation, it's important to listen, too. Leave plenty of time for silent listening when you pray a colloquy.

With the examen, imaginative prayer, and the colloquy, we have ways to make our prayer real, personal, and immediate as the Exercises proceed.

Chapter 4

It's Not about You

The First Principle and Foundation

What brings people to the Spiritual Exercises? What brings *you*? Why are you reading this book?

I have a friend who's lost. He's an accountant with a good job; he lives with his wife and two teenage daughters in a comfortable home. He goes to church and enjoys sports and fishing and golf. A fine, respectable life—on the surface. My friend worries about losing his job; his marriage disappoints him; he complains about not being able to talk to his kids. He's bored most of the time. Sometimes he's depressed. Every few months he takes a couple of hundred dollars out of the bank and goes to the casino. He feels most alive at the black-jack table, trying to outwit the dealer by counting cards. He's the guy Bob Dylan interrogated in one of his great songs:

"How does it feel / To be on your own / With no direction home / Like a complete unknown / Like a rolling stone?"

A spiritual director I know says that most people who come to the Exercises are stuck in a spiritual rut. They want more—more of life and more of God. They wonder: Is this as good as it gets? They're asking the questions that most of us start asking in our early twenties and that never really go away: What am I doing here? What's the point? I've got a good mind, a fine education, a steady job, lots of nice things, so why, then, do I feel so restless, like a rolling stone, with no direction home? These are the feelings that bring people to the Spiritual Exercises.

The Big Picture

Ignatius lays down a couple of prerequisites for people interested in making the Exercises. One is that we enter them "with magnanimity and generosity toward [our] Creator and Lord." This is a pretty general requirement. It means that, at the very least, we come with the spirit of openness, not suspicion. But it means more than that. Magnanimity and generosity imply eagerness, enthusiasm, and zeal for what's to come.

The other requirement is that we buy into something called "the First Principle and Foundation," a big-picture understanding of where we stand with God. Most of us like to have a goal in mind when we start new ventures. We look at the business plan, the table of contents, the syllabus. Every training program, workshop, or course of treatment, such as physical therapy, starts with the setting of goals. Not so with the Spiritual Exercises. Ignatius didn't know what the outcome of the Exercises would be for anyone. Remember his guideline for spiritual directors: "Permit the Creator to deal directly with the creature, and the creature directly with his Creator and Lord." But he does set forth some basic principles. He's like a choir director passing out the sheet music. Each of us will sing in our own way, but Ignatius wants to make sure that we're singing the same song. The message of the First Principle and Foundation is that we're *not* on our own, with no direction home, like a rolling stone.

The language of the First Principle and Foundation is unlike anything else in the Exercises. It's a mixture of catechism definitions and philosophical assertion.

> Man is created to praise, reverence, and serve God our Lord, and by this means to save his soul. The other things on the face of the earth are created for man to help him in attaining the end for which he is created.

Hence, man is to make use of them in as far as they help him in the attainment of his end, and he must rid himself of them in as far as they prove a hindrance to him.

Therefore, we must make ourselves indifferent to all created things, as far as we are allowed free choice and are not under any prohibition. Consequently, as far as we are concerned, we should not prefer health to sickness, riches to poverty, honor to dishonor, a long life to a short one. The same holds for all other things.

Our one desire and choice should be what is more conducive to the end for which we are created.

The Spiritual Exercises reach for our affective powers—our emotions and feelings. But the First Principle and Foundation is aimed specifically at our intellect. Ignatius wants us to *understand* certain things about God's creative purpose and the place of human beings within it.

The Challenge of Life

Man is created to praise, reverence, and serve God our Lord. In other words, it's not about you. It's about God; specifically, it's about a relationship between you and God. We're created to love God, and God gave us everything we see around us—the "things on the face of the earth"—to help us do that. God is a creative lover. You might say that God is love, loving. If you think that God loves you only when you're a good person who follows the rules, then you'll see life as a time of testing in which you work hard to do the right thing and stay out of trouble. If you see creation as a gift to help you "know God more easily," then you'll see life as a way of growing closer to God.

Another implication of the big picture: God is *here*, working in this world, present to us in an infinite number of ways. It's like a giant satellite TV with a thousand channels. One of the great themes of Ignatian spirituality is "finding God in all things." Other spiritualities emphasize one or two of these channels, such as fixed-hour prayer, fasting, solitude, devotional practices, and self-denial. Ignatian spirituality looks for God in everything. It's the difference between a silent movie in black and white and a high-speed Internet connection bringing us a million websites.

If this is true—if our work, relationships, and the other things on the face of the earth are ways to know God—then the choices we make about these things are just about the most important things we do. As the First Principle and Foundation puts it, the goal is to "choose what better leads to God's deepening life in me." The challenge of life is to choose the good and avoid the bad. The objects of our choices are "the other things on the face of the earth"—the work we do, our friends and family, our responsibilities, our ambitions and hopes and disappointments, the opportunities and misfortunes that come our way. In other words, everything. All of it is meaningful. Nothing is so small, so fleeting, so distasteful, or so awful that it's excluded from God's love.

Choosing well is easier said than done. It's easy to get off track, to make poor choices, to make choices for the wrong reasons, or to get bogged down in a muddle of conflicting desires and the infinite variety of possible futures available to us. Perhaps the most common mistake is doing it backward. Instead of putting God first and then choosing the course that brings us closer to God, we often choose what seems best to us and then try to fit God into that. You might choose the career that seems to suit you—and then ask God to bless it. You might decide to get married—and then ask God to make the marriage a success. These might not necessarily be *bad* decisions, but Ignatius says that the *best* decisions begin by us asking what will bring us closer to God.

What Indifference Means

How do we make good choices? The answer to this question is one of the most surprising and novel ideas in the Exercises. A literal translation of the First Principle and Foundation puts it this way: "we must make ourselves *indifferent* to all created things." The contemporary paraphrase says "we must hold ourselves *in balance* before all created gifts." Another word for *indifference* is *freedom*. Ignatius says that to make good decisions, we must try to be free from personal preferences, societal expectations, fear of poverty and loneliness, desire for fame and honor, and anything else that stands in the way of the choice that will best serve God and bring us true happiness. These are the disordered attachments that Ignatius wants us to be free of.

Ignatius puts it in stark, even shocking, terms. He says (in the literal translation), "We should not prefer health to sickness, riches to poverty, honor to dishonor, a long life to a short life." I confess that Ignatius's language here put me off when I first read it. It seemed extreme (and psychologically impossible) not to care whether I was sick or healthy. But Ignatius's point is about taking a good, hard, and honest look at the motives that shape our lives. He's saying that we shouldn't allow concerns for our physical well-being, reputation, or financial security to control us. Remember, we're talking about decisions and choices that shape our lives. We're not talking about likes and dislikes in the abstract. No one likes to be sick, and, to quote Woody Allen, "Money is better than poverty, if only for financial reasons." The problem comes when these things direct our lives. We all know people whose lives are centered on working out and eating healthy food; people who take a bad job to make money; people who strut and preen, hoping to be noticed; people whose lives revolve around sex or bass fishing or shopping or collecting classic cars. The conventional wisdom about life choices is to follow your bliss. Ignatius wouldn't disagree, as long as your bliss is what you truly want, and not some cheap substitute that we choose for ourselves independent of God.

Usually, it's quite difficult to sort out the confusing muddle of ordered and disordered attachments that most of us live with. When does a desire to be liked and complimented become abnormal vanity? I need money to live; I have a mortgage and a car that's breaking down. I'd also like some new clothes, a remodeled kitchen, and a vacation. How much more money do I need? What I am I willing to do to get it? We begin to answer these difficult questions by starting from a position of freedom—detachment from any particular outcome, from other people's ideas of the good life, from considerations of how someone like you *should* act.

Achieving this kind of freedom greatly helped a friend of mine, Brian, who made the Spiritual Exercises because he had a restless sense that he should open up to something new. Brian was a tenured professor of psychology at a small liberal arts college. He enjoyed his work, students liked him, and he was getting some attention for his research in new instructional technologies. During the Exercises, Brian thought about why he did the work he was doing, and he came to see that he greatly valued the security and prestige that came with his tenured faculty position. There's nothing wrong with that, but Brian looked for a deeper passion to motivate his life. In time he found it—not in the classroom but in the ideas he had for using the Web for college instruction. A year after he did the Exercises, Brian resigned his position and launched a start-up company that designs online courses for colleges and universities. The new job was a lot less secure; many of his friends thought his decision made no sense. But it made sense to Brian, who discovered what he *really* wanted. He found his deepest desire by committing himself to Christ and trusting that Christ would show him the way to go.

When he talks about indifference, Ignatius really means it. You might think that an aristocrat who gave up his wealth to embrace a life of poverty and celibacy would think that others should imitate him. Not so. For Ignatius, indifference means that you are as ready to choose a life of comfort as a life of hardship. The free person's only desire is to become the person God meant him or her to be.

That means that every walk of life can be a way to God. As the Jesuit poet Gerard Manley Hopkins put it: "To lift up the hands in prayer gives God glory, but a man with a dung fork in his hand, a woman with a slop pail, gives him glory too." It also means that you don't have to be afraid. That's what Ignatius told a Jesuit who feared for his spiritual well-being in the snake pit of intrigue and dissipation at the royal court where he worked. Your calling is to be with these people and serve them, Ignatius wrote. If you are faithful to your calling, then you have nothing to fear. "Christ himself" will look after you.

The preliminaries are over. We've learned new methods of prayer, and Ignatius has set out the big picture: this is not about you; it's about God in your life. Let the Exercises begin.

Chapter 5

Loved Sinners

The Mystery of Sin

One night Jesus was dining at a Pharisee's home when a woman suddenly entered the room. She was a "public sinner," perhaps a euphemism for a prostitute. Weeping, she approached Jesus and let her tears fall on his feet. She wiped his feet with her hair, kissed them, and anointed them with costly oil from an alabaster flask. Simon, the Pharisee host, observed this moving scene with a heart of stone and sarcastically commented that Jesus couldn't be much of a prophet if he didn't know that the woman touching him was a sinner. Jesus knew. So did the woman. Jesus explained: "Her many sins have been forgiven; hence, she has shown great love."

The scene at the Pharisee's dinner table shows us everything we need to know about sin. We see heartfelt sorrow and great love, human repentance and divine forgiveness. The scene depicts one of the greatest of the many paradoxes and mysteries of the Christian faith. God has high hopes for us, yet God forgives us when we fall short. We fail, yet God looks upon us with love. We also see moral blindness in this scene. Simon the Pharisee is blind to the woman's repentance and to Jesus' love and forgiveness. The woman is dismayed by her sinfulness; Simon can't see his. He has no idea what is going on.

That's the problem Ignatius seeks to remedy in the first "week," or section, of the Exercises. When it comes to sin, we have no idea what is going on. At best we have a glimmer of an idea. We might think, "Mistakes were made," or in a moment of great candor say, "I screwed up." Ignatius leads us through an honest stocktaking, a coming to grips with sin and failure, a recognition of how much we need from God.

Love Comes First (and Last, and Always)

The first week of the Exercises consists of five meditations on sin, beginning with sin considered as an objective reality and continuing on to a searching examination of our own sinfulness and its consequences. We're invited to recall our own history of sin in concrete particulars—the times and places, the people involved, the deeds and misdeeds. We ponder the grim fact that we are surrounded by sin, evil, and death and are inevitably affected by it. Most people find this difficult; I certainly did.

It's possible to do it only because of the love of God. The image that looms over the first week is the dying Jesus nailed to the cross. The crucifix depicts the greatest evil and the greatest love, a monstrous crime and the act that delivers us from the clutches of that crime. Before we look at our personal history of sin, Ignatius has us come before the crucifix and ask, "What have I done for Christ? What am I doing for Christ? What ought I to do for Christ?" The crucifix reminds us of God's overwhelming love, which makes it possible for us to look at our sin and be freed from it. Ignatius's questions remind us that the point of all this is to respond to God's love. Ignatius doesn't ask us to look at the sorry state of the world and the messes we've made so that we can feel bad. We do this so that we can do the deeds of love: ask for and receive forgiveness, and be freed to serve Christ more faithfully.

There's another sense in which love comes first. We wouldn't know much about sin unless God told us about it. The woman at the Pharisee's house wept bitter tears because God's love opened her eyes to the truth about her life. Sin isn't the human condition; it's the *explanation* for the human condition. Without knowledge of sin, life makes no sense at all.

A Tale Told by an Idiot

I first got a glimmer of this when I was a sophomore in high school. The occasion was the first live play I had ever seen: a production of *Macbeth* in a high school gym in Bergen-field, New Jersey. The humdrum setting took nothing away from the theatrical power of Shakespeare's tale of betrayal, witchcraft, insanity, and murder. I was completely caught up in it. I was right *there* as the disasters of Act V unfolded: the unholy vision, Lady Macbeth's madness, her suicide, and Macbeth's soliloquy of bitter despair as bloody doom descends on him:

> Life's but a walking shadow, a poor player
> That struts and frets his hour upon the stage
> And then is heard no more. It is a tale
> Told by an idiot, full of sound and fury,
> Signifying nothing.

Mind you, nobody talked like this in the snug pre-Vatican II, East Coast, Irish-Catholic cocoon that I grew up in. Nobody thought like this either, as far as I knew. But that night I realized that some people did. Art worked its magic and caused me to understand a couple of things. I understood how Macbeth would think that life was meaningless, and through him I glimpsed the landscape of a world without God and without a purpose, without an explanation of why things are the way they are. But I also understood something Macbeth didn't: his wicked deeds had caused this bloody catastrophe. Things looked bad because he had made them that way.

Time passed, my education continued, and I learned that Macbeth's attitude was pretty much the prevailing view of twentieth-century intellectuals. I read Albert Camus ("the one truly serious philosophical problem is suicide") and James Joyce ("history is a nightmare from which I am trying to awake"). I read Jean-Paul Sartre ("We want to anesthetize ourselves; we do not want to realize that underneath all of this there is nothingness. When we realize that, the only proper attitude is despair and tremendous anxiety.").

This picture changes considerably when we learn that the world is a sorry mess because it's alienated from God. We've lost our way. We're wandering in the wilderness, trying to find our way home. Amazingly, sin becomes a source of hope. It explains why things fall apart, why we do things we hate, why we struggle to do the right thing, why we suffer at the hands of people doing the wrong things. Sin shows us that history is not simply a nightmare and that we don't need to stare into a void with tremendous anxiety. Things don't have to be this way. We can hope for a better world because this world isn't the world that God intended. Sin shows us that life as we know it isn't a meaningless tale told by an idiot. Rather, our lives are broken, and they need to be fixed.

I wasn't taught about the hopeful side of sin during my years of religious education. Many of the nuns and brothers who taught me in school had a bleak view of the human condition. They tended toward the opinion of St. Augustine, who thought that humanity was a *massa damnata*—a huge mass of doomed souls, rebellious and ignorant, headed for hell. In the Augustinian view, God bestows the graces of salvation sparingly. Ignatius saw it differently. He understood how pervasive sin is, but he also saw how freely God bestows his grace. In the Exercises, Ignatius describes God bathing us with blessings, like the sun shining on the earth, like a fountain flowing with an endless stream of water. All is grace—even sin is grace.

Sin Makes Us Stupid

A kid named Larry liked to ask challenging questions in my freshman high school religion class. He was bright and articulate; teachers regarded him as something of a smart aleck, but you couldn't dismiss him as a mischief maker because there was often a serious point to his questions. One day the brother who was teaching the class was talking about Jesus' prayer from the cross, "Father, forgive them; for they do not know what they are doing." Larry piped up, "Why should God forgive those people if they don't know what they are doing?"

Pretty good question. In class we'd learned that certain conditions had to be met to make a sin mortal, and one of them was that the sinner had to *know* that the deed was seriously wrong. So if the people killing Jesus thought they were doing the right thing, why did God need to forgive them? I forget what the teacher said; I was too busy admiring the clever spitball Larry had lobbed into the lap of authority. I can see now that we were working with a seriously deficient definition of sin—that sin was largely a matter of breaking rules. If you didn't know the rule, you couldn't sin. Sin is a lot more complicated than that. Still, Larry had a point. In the secular world, ignorance of the law is no excuse. But in religion, might not ignorance get you off the hook?

Not really, because sin makes us stupid. The Bible is full of sinners who didn't know they were doing wrong. In fact, they thought that their wrongdoing was right. The people who killed Jesus thought they were keeping order in the land and protecting the faith. The prodigal son's older brother thought he was right to be angry because his father's mercy had offended justice. The Pharisees were sure, absolutely sure, that healing people on the Sabbath was wrong. The people of Israel were expressing real religious needs when they worshipped idols. The world is full of people like this. The adulterer, the terrorist, the spiteful neighbor, the drug dealer, the aunt who won't talk to anyone in the family—all of them have reasons to do what they're doing, reasons that make sense to them. But sin has clouded their minds; they don't see the obvious. Isn't that what you think when you see people doing outrageous things, like spreading malicious rumors, destroying their families and careers in pursuit of sex, or concocting schemes to steal people's money? You think, *Someone should tell these people that this is wrong!*

We've all heard the little voice in our heads justifying acts that don't seem quite right: Flirting with a coworker is playful fun. Getting drunk is just blowing off steam. Spreading ugly gossip is just chitchat. Cutting corners and lying are the things you have to do in a "competitive business environment." If we can't quite justify these things, we can minimize them. "It's not so very wrong." "There are worse things." "It is what it is." Even better, we can avoid thinking about these things at all. Sin is like life insurance: too distressing to ponder. A friend of mine who sells life insurance jokes that he can drive people out of a crowded room by simply walking in the door and whispering, "Life insurance." People immediately head for the exits. It's the same with sin. Sin is negative; let's talk about something that will make us feel good about ourselves.

The scene at the Pharisee's dinner table shows something else about sin that's important. The woman who tearfully bathed Jesus' feet was likely a prostitute—someone who traffics in false love. There's a sense in which all sin is a kind of prostitution: misplaced love, a sorry substitute for the real thing. Recall what Ignatius said about disordered attachments. Our cravings for money, sex, power, and honor obscure our deepest desire, which is to find the way of life that will give us lasting peace and joy. Chasing these things is "looking for love in all the wrong places," to quote Waylon Jennings's great country-and-western song. They are not intrinsically evil; we need money to pay the bills, and there's nothing wrong with taking pride in a job well done. But when these things become the passions that drive our lives, when they become the reason we get out of bed in the morning, we're in the grip of a fantasy. We've bought a counterfeit, an illusion that looks like the real thing.

As I worked my way through the first week of the Spiritual Exercises, I came to see sin as a kind of ignorance, but an ignorance more of the heart than of the mind. Yes, it's crazy to simultaneously worry about what other people think about me and feel sorry for myself because they're *not* thinking about me. Of course it makes no sense to complain about the few things I don't have and ignore the many things God has given me. Sure, it's perverse to alienate people I love by pressing my opinions and judgments on them. But I like my opinions, my self-pity feels good, and my delusions of mastery are great fun, so I do these things anyway. That's why Ignatius isn't much interested in getting us to *understand* sin. He wants us to *feel* it with our hearts so that we can fall in love with the right things.

"We Have Met the Enemy and He Is Us"

"I am the problem"—that's a line from the journal I kept as I made the Exercises. Walt Kelly said it better in the famous aphorism from the *Pogo* comic strip: "We have met the enemy and he is us." Sinful actions aren't the problem.

The problem isn't so much the corners I cut or the harsh judgments I make. The problem is that I am the kind of person who cuts corners and makes harsh judgments. *I* am the problem. Sin was easier to manage when I thought it was a matter of breaking rules. But sinful actions aren't the core of what's wrong. Lies, stealing, angry tirades, and all the rest arise from deep disorders within. Our "sin problem" isn't the bad things we do that violate moral laws. The problem, as the Jesuit Joseph Tetlow put it, is "the fact that I am from a dysfunctional family, work in a dysfunctional job, am surrounded by neurotics, with whom I fit perfectly." The worst thing is seeing how I fall short of my own ideals. I *know* how to act; I just don't act that way. St. Paul said it in words that everyone can relate to: "I do not understand my own actions. For I do not do what I want, but I do the very thing I hate."

So I try to take seriously the idea that sin makes us dense and stupid. I'm not sure I know what sin is, so I'm skeptical when people say they do, particularly when they say that there's not much of it around. It's great that we're aware of the ways that bad parenting, addictions, betrayals, trauma, advertising, sibling rivalry, and unconscious striving for our father's approval shape our behavior. But I'm not so sure that people are being enlightened when they minimize bad behavior ("a joke that went too far"), rename it ("something he had to do"), trivialize it ("a phase"), or privatize it ("between consenting adults"). I'm also skeptical when people are sure that they know what other people's sins are, but that's a topic for another time.

Another line from my journal is "sin is a mystery," something that Dennis said one day. It's a mystery that things are the way they are. It's a mystery because it defies logic and common sense that people repeatedly behave in ways contrary to their best interests, and that they do so without really wanting to. It's also a mystery in the sense that it's something beyond human comprehension. God's creation is good, yet it's corrupted by sin. God is omniscient and omnipotent, yet we have the freedom to do what we want. God is just yet all-loving. All this is true, but *how* all this is true is a puzzle indeed. Because sin is a mystery, we need to ask God to enlighten us. Sin is blindness too.

A Gratitude Deficit

Ignatius thought that a particular type of ignorance was at the root of sin. The deadliest sin, he said, is ingratitude. It is "the cause, beginning, and origin of all evils and sins." If you asked a hundred people to name the sin that's the origin of all evils, I'll bet none of them would say ingratitude. They would say pride or disobedience or greed or anger. The idea that we sin because we're not sufficiently aware of God's goodness probably wouldn't occur to too many people.

Gratitude meant something different in Ignatius's time from what it does today. Gratitude to us means sending thank-you notes for Christmas presents or thanking neighbors when they give us a hand. For us, ingratitude is something like bad manners. Gratitude was a much more serious matter in Ignatius's late-medieval society, which was organized around a set of mutual obligations among those in social and political hierarchies. Everyone needed to be aware of the contributions of everyone else. Gratitude was the glue that bound people together. But cultural differences are only part of the story. By emphasizing gratitude, Ignatius was saying something about the nature of God. God is the generous giver, showering us with blessings like the sun shining on the earth. If we truly understood this, we would return God's love with love. We wouldn't sin. *Gratitude* is a good word for this fundamental quality of our relationship with God. Ingratitude, our blindness to who God truly is, is thus the root of all sin.

Ignatius had a particular experience of sin that may have contributed to the high value he placed on gratitude. For a time, he was tormented by morbid scrupulosity. He didn't think his sins had been forgiven, so he tried to drive out his guilt and shame with heroic ascetic practices. He fasted, he prayed for hours, he let his hair grow—but these things only made matters worse. It got so bad that he entertained thoughts of suicide. Eventually, Ignatius threw himself on God's mercy and found peace. He saw himself as a sinner but as a loved sinner.

In his short story "The Repentant Sinner," Leo Tolstoy tells of a man, a great sinner, who calls out to God for mercy just before he dies. He arrives at the gates of heaven, but they are locked. The apostle Peter explains that a sinner such as he can't enter heaven, but the man reminds Peter of *his* sins—he denied Christ three times after swearing to be loyal. Peter goes away and is replaced by King David, who also says that sinners can't enter heaven. The man reminds David that God had mercy on *him* despite his many sins, including adultery and murder. Finally the apostle John arrives. "You are the beloved disciple," the man says. "You wrote that 'God is love' and 'Brethren, love one another.' Surely, you must let me in." And sure enough, John embraces the man and escorts him into heaven.

That's the purpose of the first week of the Exercises—to bring us to see that we are loved sinners. Seasoned preachers and speakers know that they've done a good job if people can take away one idea from their talk. If you take away one idea from the Spiritual Exercises, this is the one: *you are a sinner who is loved by God.*

But there's more. The God who loves us has work for us to do.

Chapter 6

There's Work to Be Done

The Call of the King

I'm afflicted with enthusiasm deficit disorder. I've been inspired by great leaders and invested hope and energy in great causes, but the leaders always turn out to be human beings like everybody else, and the fervor always leaks away when the causes meet opposition and complexity. Every time that happens, my enthusiasm deficit deepens.

I felt this disappointment for the first time when I was a young newspaper reporter fresh out of college at the height of the Vietnam War. I got to know the leaders of an antiwar organization headquartered in the New York suburb that was part of my beat. I greatly admired these young men and women. They seemed to be smart, idealistic, and selfless; many were motivated by a strong religious faith. (Hey, they were a lot like *me*!) My admiration faded as I got to know them better. They didn't like one another very much. The organization's internal politics were nasty. They didn't work together very well. They made good speeches and wrote fine press releases, but they didn't get much done. (They really *were* a lot like me.) This pattern was repeated several times over the years. I'd get excited about a program for change or reform or renewal, and then the project would founder, often because of the personal failings of the people in charge. "Reality always wins," says a cynical friend.

Enthusiasm deficit disorder was foreign to Ignatius. He was an activist. Ignatian spirituality sees Christ hard at work in the world—bringing justice, healing the sick, feeding the hungry, forgiving sins, and comforting the grieving—and asks us to do the same. The Ignatian motto, "find God in all things," means that God is to be found within creation, not outside it. God is active, ever-present, prodding, suggesting, inviting. One meditation in the Spiritual Exercises asks us to consider how God "conducts himself as one who labors." Our God is a busy God, and we're called to get busy, too. This idea is as old as the great commission in Matthew's Gospel: "Go therefore and make disciples of all nations."

Not all Christians are activists in the Ignatian mold. In the history of the church, the spirit of activism has coexisted with a yearning for solitude and prayer. The Christian monastic movement dates from the sixth century, when St. Benedict of Nursia gathered men into monastic communities as the Roman Empire collapsed. Monastic communities preserved Christianity through centuries of turmoil. The turmoil has never ended, and neither has the desire to retreat from it. Some contemporary Christians would like to see the church take what's called the "Benedict option," an extended period of retreat and purification in the face of an increasingly hostile climate for believers. In this way, Christians would form communities that stand apart from the world and try to inspire others by example rather than by engagement.

Neo-Benedictine communities may well have a place in the church (almost *everything* has a place in the church), but they wouldn't be at the core of an Ignatian program for Christian mission. Ignatius's attitude clearly favors engagement rather than retreat. The symbol of Ignatian engagement might be a life-size crucifix in a church in Germany that shows the familiar body of Jesus except for one thing: Jesus has no arms. The statue was damaged in World War II, and when the parishioners repaired it they decided to leave the arms off to remind themselves that *they* are Christ's arms. A wonderful expression of this idea is the poem

"Christ Has No Body" by St. Teresa of Ávila (who had several Jesuit spiritual directors). The poem begins:

> Christ has no body but yours,
> No hands, no feet on earth but yours,
> Yours are the eyes with which he looks
> Compassion on this world.

Ignatius didn't invent Christian engagement in the world, but he certainly emphasized it. A major goal of the Spiritual Exercises is finding the work God has for each of us to do. This theme wends its way through the Exercises, and it begins with the meditation Call of the King.

Of Kings and Infidels

If you need a reminder that the *Spiritual Exercises* were written in a time and place very different from today, you'll get it from the Call of the King exercise, which begins the second week of the Exercises. Ignatius asks us to imagine an immensely powerful and terrifically charismatic earthly king inviting us to join him in his work of conquering "all the lands of the infidel." We will work alongside this great king, sharing the same food and drink and shelter. We will do great work together and share in a great victory. Ignatius takes it for granted that we'll accept such an invitation.

Then we're to imagine that this king is Christ, and that he's personally inviting us to join him in his work in the world. Christ says, "whoever wishes to join me in this enterprise must be willing to labor with me, that by following me in suffering, he may follow me in glory." If the earthly king's words thrilled us, we'll be even more excited about signing up with Christ the King. At least that's the way the exercise is supposed to work, and in sixteenth-century Europe, maybe it did.

Today this exercise needs cultural translation. The only king in America is Elvis, and to speak of infidels is extremely politically incorrect, so I tried to capture the spirit of the exercise by thinking about the inspiring kings I had known—British kings. I went to YouTube and watched a clip from the movie *Henry V* from Shakespeare's play, the scene where the king, played by Kenneth Branagh, rallies his men before the Battle of Agincourt ("We few, we happy few, we band of brothers; / For he to-day that sheds his blood with me / Shall be my brother"). I got chills when I watched this scene on the big screen in the movie theater, and I got chills seeing it again on my laptop screen. Henry's words moved me. I could imagine following a man like that (although not into a bloody, senseless slaughter like the Battle of Agincourt).

Then I thought about King George VI, played by Colin Firth in the movie *The King's Speech*, struggling courageously to overcome a crippling speech defect. The point of the movie hinges on understanding why it was important that the king of England be able to speak well in a time of war. The king symbolizes the entire nation. In a sense, he embodies the whole people. If the king was strong and hopeful in times of trouble, then the nation was strong and hopeful, too. If the king looked weak, inarticulate, and fumbling, then something was wrong with the nation as well.

Both Henry V and George VI capture something of what a king meant to Ignatius. Ignatius is tapping into something deep in the human psyche in his Call of the King exercise. Almost all cultures have a myth of a great king who will right all wrongs, bring justice to the realm, rule with wisdom, and vanquish enemies. The people of Israel longed for a successor to King David. Britons pined for the return of King Arthur. Yearning for a good king is part of the appeal of Tolkien's Lord of the Rings and other popular fantasy sagas. Ignatius wants us to feel this yearning viscerally. He is saying, *Jesus is the One*—the new Moses, the new David. Try to read the Call of the King exercise with a sense of eager joy that the longed-for leader is speaking to you personally.

Singing in the Gospel Choir

First comes the call, then the response. Christ calls us, we answer. The pattern of call-and-response lies deep in our psyches. It's a basic pattern of religion, literature, and sports. It's especially pronounced in music. You can hear call and respone in folk music, jazz, and rock and roll, in monastic choirs and gospel choirs. It's as old as the psalms and as up to date as a contemporary pop song. If you've seen the movie *Casablanca*, you might remember the call-and-response riff between Sam and the band in the song "Knock on Wood":

Who's got trouble?
We've got trouble!
How much trouble?
Too much trouble!

The really interesting part of the Call of the King exercise is what Ignatius has to say about our response to Christ's call. We might respond in two different ways. One way is the "reasonable" response. What would a normal, sensible person do upon hearing an invitation to join a great leader in an effort to bring peace, justice, and prosperity to the world? *Of course* you'd sign up. Who wouldn't? Ignatius writes, "All persons who have judgment and reason will offer themselves entirely for this work." Perhaps we can't assume that response today, an age full of reforming visionaries offering plans to people afflicted with enthusiasm deficit disorder, so let's adapt the exercise a bit. A very talented and capable leader personally invites you to join an effort to feed the hungry in your community. The need is acute; the remedy is practical; the hungry need your help. Of course you would support such a program. You would at least write a check. You might tell your friends about it. You might buy a ticket to a fund-raising dinner.

But you could go further—much further. You could become a volunteer and solicit donations. You could collect food and deliver it to hungry people. You might join the board of the organization and lobby public officials to support programs to feed the hungry. You could retire or quit your job and spend all your time on efforts to get food to hungry people. Feeding the hungry could become the thing that gets you out of bed in the morning. This is the second kind of response we might make to the call of the king, and it's the answer Ignatius wants us to consider: we might become people who will "offer themselves entirely for this work." Ignatius goes even further than "entirely." He speaks of people who will "give *greater* proof of their love," who will act against their natural inclinations and "make offerings of *greater* value." People who want this will be willing even to suffer the same abuse and rejection that Christ suffered and to endure actual poverty, so that they can give all they have.

This is the famous *magis* of Ignatian spirituality. *Magis* is a Latin word meaning "more." It's been called the Jesuit "itch"—an ambition to reach greater heights, to conquer new frontiers, to maintain even higher standards. *Magis* is sometimes associated with restless type A overachieving, but the word has more to do with the quality of our personal commitment to Christ than with long hours and a crowded schedule. Christ loves us without limit. Of course we love him in return, but when we strive for the magis we're always looking for what *more* we can do to express that love.

The *magis* is quite daunting. When I was reflecting on the Call of the King, I was reminded of the rich young man who approached Jesus and asked what he could do to inherit eternal life. Jesus asked him if he loved God and loved his neighbor—the basic commandments that all good Jews were to observe. The man answered that he did, and he asked what more he could do. Jesus "looked at him with love" and invited him to give away all his possessions and join Jesus' itinerant band of fishermen, tax collectors, outcasts, and society's fringe dwellers. Jesus offered him the *magis*. The rich young man declined—no surprise, I thought. To be honest, I would probably decline, too.

"Make a competent and sufficient effort"

There's an old saying that we should "pray as if everything depends on God, work as if everything depends on you." It's been attributed to Ignatius (though there's no evidence that he ever said it), and many think that the formula captures the Ignatian spirit: turning everything over to God in prayer and then working tirelessly and urgently to do God's work. I think it's better to reverse the saying: "pray as if everything depends on you, work as if everything depends on God." This means that prayer, not work, has to be urgent; if everything depends on *me,* God had better show up! It also puts our work in the right perspective; if the success of our work depends on God, we can let it go. If God is in charge, we can tolerate mixed results and endure failure.

Failure and disappointment are sure to come. Any project that involves human beings will fall short somewhere. Consider those antiwar activists in New York I met when I was a young reporter. At the time, I was disappointed to discover that the group's leaders had unlikable personal qualities. Today I have a more seasoned perspective (I hope), and

I can see that the group's problems were nothing special. Every group has shortcomings, and every person has flaws. The Ignatian perspective allows little room for illusions and utopian dreams. Yes—Christ is working to save and heal the world, but we're not going to see heaven on earth.

There are no guarantees. Next time you find yourself slipping into grandiosity or excessive optimism, ponder these words about "Christian failure" by the Jesuit theologian Walter Burghardt:

> Just because I am trying to do God's work with every ounce of my being is no guarantee that my plans will prosper. There is no guarantee that an effective Christian disciple will not be cut down in his prime. There is no guarantee that because you have given yourself to a Christian marriage, your oneness will be lasting. That because you love God deeply, you will not lose your job, your home, your family, your health. There is no guarantee that because you believe, you will not doubt; because you hope, you will not despond; because you love, your love will not grow cold.

But read the rest of it, too:

> You do your Christian task as God gives you; the rest, the increase, is in His hands. God still uses what the world calls foolish to shame the wise, still uses what the world calls weak to shame its strength, still uses what the world calls

low and insignificant and unreal to nullify its realities. In this sense, there is no Christian frustration and no Christian failure.

Ignatius wrote about work and human effort in a letter to an aristocrat named Jerome Vines, whom I imagine was a busy, hard-charging, type A character who was getting upset about the fate of his many projects. A busy man, Ignatius writes, "must make up his mind to do what he can, without afflicting himself if he cannot do all that he wishes. You must have patience and not think that God our Lord requires what man cannot accomplish." He concludes with this: "There is no need to wear yourself out, but make a competent and sufficient effort, and leave the rest to him who can do all he pleases."

Many times in the Call of the King exercise, Christ invites us to work *with* him: "join with me," "work with me," "watch with me," "share in the toil with me," "share in the victory with me." Christ isn't some distant leader making eloquent speeches. He's a leader who throws himself into the work, who gets down into the trenches, who gets his hands dirty, who goes hungry, and who sleeps in a tent. The Call of the King exercise helped me see that the work I do is a way of coming to know Christ. For me, this has been one of the lasting gifts of the Spiritual Exercises.

The Call of the King exercise isn't about shoulds or ought-tos. It's an exercise, a scenario, an act of the imagination that probes where you are and suggests possible new directions. One possible direction is an unreserved, all-in, no-holds-barred response to Christ's invitation to join him in his work of healing the world. Ignatius isn't saying you *should* respond this way, or even that you *can*. It's an option. Is it the right answer for you? We'll see.

You've heard the call. In the next meditation, you'll ponder what answering the call might entail.

Chapter 7

"You're Gonna Have to Serve Somebody"

The Two Standards

A Jesuit at my parish, a linguist and a Scripture scholar, goes to every Bob Dylan concert he can. He'll drive hundreds of miles, rearrange his vacations, and stand in line in the rain to get tickets. Some of this passion is nostalgia for his younger days; "Dylan is the troubadour of my generation," he says. Much of it is pure enjoyment of the concert experience. But a good part of it is attraction to Dylan's spiritual concerns. Dylan is a spiritually sensitive man, and you'll find religious imagery in many of his songs, such as "All Along the Watchtower" and "Ring Them Bells" ("Ring them bells, sweet Martha, for the poor man's son, ring them bells so the world will know that God is one"). One of my favorites is the song "Gotta Serve Somebody." Dylan drives home the message: "You're gonna have to serve somebody." You can't avoid it. Everybody serves—gamblers, diplomats, rock stars, cops, construction workers, everybody. "It may be the devil or it may be the Lord, but you're gonna have to serve somebody." You'll dance to somebody's tune. You'll please a master, and you'll come to value what your master values and think how your master thinks.

You've already heard the Call of the King. The Two Standards, another imaginative meditation during the second week of the Exercises, will take you more deeply into the implications of the call you're answering. In this exercise, we're to imagine two armies gathered around standards, or battle flags. One army is led by Satan, "the deadly enemy of our human nature," seated on a great throne of fire and smoke. Satan sends demons to all the ends of the earth with instructions to lead humans to ruin through desire for riches, honor, and pride. The second army is led by Christ, who sends his disciples out into the world to invite people to a life of poverty, rejection, and humility. Two masters with two very different value systems are vying for your allegiance, and you have to choose one or the other.

Didn't Mother Teresa Deserve Her Nobel Prize?

When I first read this meditation, I thought it was pretty simple stuff, even a bit simplistic. Jesus on the one hand, and Satan on the other hand—make your choice. The choice is obvious. But it's not simple at all. For starters, the exercise presents neither good nor evil in their most obvious forms. Satan doesn't work through hatred, anger, and jealousy; he tempts us to riches and honor. These are not evil things in themselves. They can even be good. Wasn't Mother Teresa's Nobel Peace Prize a well-deserved honor? Don't wealthy people use their money to support many good works?

The same is true for Christ's program. He doesn't invite his followers to lives of kindness, mercy, and love. He offers poverty, obscurity, and humility. These aren't necessarily bad things, but they're not very attractive either. In fact, they can be quite undesirable. The poverty that afflicts so many millions of people is an evil to be fought, not a virtue to be embraced. It's an odd message, like people looking for romance on a matchmaking website describing themselves as plain and serious instead of fun loving and sexy.

Behind this meditation is a practical theory of vice and virtue. Good and evil aren't abstractions. They show themselves in concrete actions in the real world. Note a couple of significant details in the meditation. First, the contest between Christ and Satan takes place in this world, not in some spiritual realm. As far as we're concerned, the power of evil is centered on earth, not in hell, and God's kingdom is in this world, not in heaven. Note also that both Christ and Satan work through agents. Satan sends out demons; Christ works through apostles, disciples, and other emissaries. Another detail: no part of the earth is left out. "No province, no place, no state of life, no individual is overlooked." You don't get a pass if you're a priest or nun, if you come from a religious family, or if you live in a nation with a strong Christian culture. Everybody's in this battle and must choose a side.

Even more interesting is Ignatius's idea of how virtue and vice develop. One thing leads to another. You slide down the slope to vice, or you ascend the heights to virtue. This is Satan's instructions to his minions: "They are to tempt them to covet riches . . . that they may the more easily attain the empty honors of this world, and then come to overweening pride." It's a progression: "From these three steps the evil one leads to all the other vices."

Christ also starts with riches, but he goes in the other direction. This is how his servants are to proceed: "first by attracting them to the highest spiritual poverty . . . Secondly, they should lead them to a desire for insults and contempt, for from these springs humility." That's the progression—first poverty, then obscurity, finally humility. "From these three steps, let them lead men to all the other virtues," Ignatius says.

Some years ago, I did some work for Prison Fellowship, the Christian ministry to prisoners and their families founded by Charles Colson. Some of the most interesting work I did was writing and editing the stories of prisoners. I remember one story in particular, an interview with a recently paroled inmate and his wife. The man was a banker who had served a term in prison for embezzlement. He described his downfall. He was a self-made man, raised in poverty, who had achieved a comfortable life for his family. But he didn't stop there; he wanted more money. He took some foolish risks that didn't work out, so he fudged some numbers to disguise the losses. Nobody noticed, and the deceptions gradually deepened. He "borrowed" money from the bank, promising to himself to repay it, but he never did. Soon, he found himself trying to manage a complex embezzlement scheme. The man said he was utterly confident that he could pull it off—right up to the moment he was arrested. It was a perfect illustration of the slide into ruin—a desire for riches leading to wrongdoing, propelled by a wild and foolish pride.

His story also illustrated the ascent to virtue—at least the beginning of it. The interviewer asked the couple when they had been happiest, and the wife replied, "Back when we were first married, before we had money." Husband and wife both laughed; they were poor again. The man said that now he wanted to live a simple life. He had reconnected with God in prison. He was a busy volunteer for Prison Fellowship. It sounded to me like he was learning something about humility.

What's Wrong with Money?

So virtue begins with poverty, and vice starts with riches. This is an uncomfortably practical way of looking at things, particularly for people like you and me who live more comfortably than 99 percent of all the people who've ever lived. We're certainly better off than the people who first heard the gospel. Most of them were peasants who were one bad harvest away from destitution. They worried about feeding their children; we complain about taxes and inflation. In the Two Standards meditation, Christ calls everyone to *spiritual* poverty and only some to *actual* poverty. But that doesn't mean that riches are perfectly OK for those of us not called to actual poverty.

Ignatius was repeating Scripture's clear message about riches: "You cannot serve God and wealth." Riches are among the deadliest spiritual dangers. Jesus' disciples were shocked when he said that it's easier for a camel to pass through a needle's eye than it is for a rich man to get to heaven. Pious Jews thought that wealth was a sign of God's favor. Jesus thought pretty much the opposite, that wealth separates us from God.

The Two Standards meditation shows us why. Satan's strategy begins with riches. "Riches" is the "stuff" of the world—money, of course, but also the things money can buy: homes, cars, time-shares, vintage wine, fine food, and assorted bling. It also includes intangible goods such as our skills, reputations, and status. This stuff is just stuff, neither good nor bad, until we assign meaning to it. If we view riches as very important—the source of our security, the focus of our efforts, the stuff that makes us who we are—then we'll seek more of them. And more. And more. But the problem isn't the stuff; it's the *longing* for the stuff. The old Catholic moral manuals called this *cupidity*—a wonderful Latin word meaning greed for money or possessions. If riches make you who you are, then you'll want more of them, which really means that you want more of yourself. Pretty soon, *you* is all you care about. The Jesuit Joseph Tetlow puts it neatly. At first you say, "Look at all this stuff I have." Then you say, "Look at me. I have all this stuff." Finally you say, "Look at *me*."

There's another problem with wealth, one we don't like to think much about. Jesus and the early church fathers seemed to think, at least at times, that wealth per se is an evil because it means that the poor are being oppressed. In the parable of Lazarus and the rich man, the rich man doesn't actively oppress the poor man Lazarus who begs at his gates, but the rich man is condemned anyway. His sin was ignoring the man's needs. Here is St. Basil, one of the early church fathers, preaching on the parable of the rich fool, who builds bigger barns when he comes into unexpected wealth:

> The bread which you hold back belongs to the hungry; the coat, which you guard in your locked storage-chests, belongs to the naked; the footwear mouldering in your closet belongs to those without shoes. The silver that you keep hidden in a safe place belongs to the one in need.

Yes, today we live in an age of Social Security, Section 8 housing, and homeless shelters. We're taxed to support the poor. Our capitalist economy spreads prosperity widely while it makes some people very rich. Things are different now. Or are they? Our rich world is full of single mothers and old people struggling to make ends meet, addicts and mentally ill people with no place to go, physically disabled people confined to their homes, crack babies, and kids in unstable foster care. They might have food to eat and a roof over their heads in our rich country, but few care about them. That's why the rich man was condemned; he ignored the poor man at his gates.

The Ascent to Virtue

Poverty is the first of three steps in Christ's program: "the first, poverty as opposed to riches; the second, insults or contempt as opposed to the honor of the world; the third, humility as opposed to pride."

Next in the ascent to virtue is "a desire for insults and contempt." Really? That sounds like overwrought religious language. If it's not, then Ignatius seems to be calling for an advanced state of spiritual development that seems out of reach for most people. I understand this step as accepting the consequences of a decision to opt out of the rat race and live a simple life. If you're spiritually poor, your values are different from most people's. You're not going to chase fame and fortune, and that means that you'll have less of those things than other people. Those who win the race for wealth and glory tend to look down on those who lose it. That's what it means to win: the winners get to think they are better than people like you.

This is how we achieve true humility—the third step in Christ's progression to virtue. Humility isn't self-abasement. It doesn't mean that you hold your tongue, never make a fuss, sit in the corner, or think that everyone is better than you. True humility is seeing things *as they really are*. The truth is that the world is full of other people with rights and needs and unique gifts and weaknesses. It's a web, a network full of ceaseless activity. You have a part to play in this great drama of life, and it's not the starring role. That's the way things really are. The idea that you're the center of things is an illusion.

Everyone Is an Egotist

As I worked my way through the Two Standards exercise, I realized how very hard it is to march under the standard of Christ. The problem isn't so much that riches are attractive (they are) or that poverty doesn't appeal to me (it doesn't). The problem is this: *I* am the center of every experience I've ever had. I look out at the world through *my* eyes, hear it with *my* ears, interpret it with *my* reason, and feel it with *my* feelings. Moralists complain about egocentricity as if it's a bad choice that truly virtuous people don't make. Well, egocentricity is an inescapable literal fact of consciousness. From the moment I wake up in the morning, it seems obvious that I am the center of things, and it makes perfect sense to interpret everything in relation to myself.

Here's a peek into my interior monologue one fine spring day:

My book group meets tonight, and I hope I'll say something smart about this book, something that will impress people. In fact, I'd better prepare something beforehand because I can't remember thinking anything particularly clever about this book.

I noticed a couple of fat people working out in the gym today. I'm glad I'm not fat like that. In fact, I think I look pretty good in my gray shorts and Prussian blue T-shirt.

There are some really rude and stupid people handling the phones in these big companies. The clerk in the accounts department in our medical group had my wife on hold for ten minutes before telling her to ignore the bill they sent. They couldn't care less.

It's really annoying the way the girl behind the counter at the drugstore gives me (and everyone) a bright "hello" when I walk in. Every time, without fail. I have to look at her, smile, and pretend to be cheerful, and say "hello" back. She doesn't mean it. She's been told to do that. It's just a tactic to let shoplifters know that they're being watched.

I have to drive to Chicago tomorrow. I really hate all the trucks on I-94 between Ann Arbor and Chicago. The state should have expanded it to a three-lane expressway long ago, but most of it is only two lanes, and that means that I get stuck behind slow trucks when they pass one another. Lots of rude truckers who hate normal drivers like me. Big polluters, those trucks. We'd have a lot fewer trucks if we had a better freight railroad system, but the government has screwed that up, too.

Craig owes me a phone call. Every time I see him, he says he's going to organize a guys' trip to Comerica Park to see the Tigers, but he never follows through. What's wrong with him?

And so it goes. This is what pride looks like, on the ground, in the trenches of daily life. Pride isn't just a tyrannical narcissist, screaming at underlings, spouses, and children, insisting on its own way. Pride is looking out at the world through the prism of *me* and finding it full of shortcomings, annoyances, and thoughtless people.

There's a whole other way of looking at things—the way of humility, seeing things as they really are. It's admiring the fat man at the gym for his courage, wondering whether I would do that if I were in his shoes, rooting for him, hoping I'll see him again. It's thanking God (and my employer) for the health insurance my family has. It's silently praising the manager of the drugstore for training the staff to greet people when they come in, to admire the young woman behind the counter who has to say "hello" hundreds of times a day and act like she means it, and to wonder at the discipline and effort that takes. It's to think about that long-distance trucker rumbling through Kalamazoo toward Kansas, away from his family five days a week, missing his son's piano recital and his daughter's soccer game, all to put food on the table and keep up the payments on his underwater house. It's giving Craig a call instead of wondering why he doesn't call me. Thinking this way is to be alive to a world full of courage and beauty, of suffering born patiently, of unceasing effort to do the right thing.

Looking at things this way isn't a sleight-of-hand trick of substituting rose-colored glasses for the clear light of reason. It's seeing the truth. It's what St. Thérèse of Lisieux was talking about when she prayed, "O my God, make me to see things as they really are, that I may not be deceived by any illusion." It's what Paul meant when he wrote, "I say to everyone among you not to think of yourself more highly than you ought to think, but to think with sober judgment." It's the point Ignatius is making in the Two Standards exercise. Judging things from the standpoint of the imperial self is an illusion. Looking at life as a marvelous gift is seeing the way things really are.

You're gonna have to serve somebody, but you get to choose your master. If you worship riches and honor, you'll never have enough. If you worship health, you'll always be sick. If you worship beauty, you'll always be ugly. If it's all about you, you'll be lonely, harassed, and anxious. If it's all about Christ and his work, you'll have a purpose in life, good work to do, and many good friends to do it with.

Chapter 8

Free at Last?

The Three Classes of People

Toward the end of his life, a friend asked Ignatius if anything worried him. Nothing, he said, but there was one thing that *might* worry him—the possibility that the pope would suppress the Society of Jesus. It didn't seem likely. Ignatius ran a growing, successful order acclaimed for its excellent schools and tireless missionary work. But the Jesuits had many enemies, some in high positions in the church, so suppression wasn't an entirely fanciful notion. Ignatius told his friend that he worried about suppression because he was sure God wanted the Jesuit order to thrive. Ignatius admitted that if the order were suppressed, it would disturb him, but he could accept even that. He said he would need fifteen minutes to compose himself, and then he would be at peace.

A year before his death, Ignatius's sangfroid was put to the test: Cardinal Gian Pietro Carafa, a powerful churchman who was no friend of the Jesuits, was elected pope. Ignatius feared that he would change the Jesuits—something that several influential cardinals in the Vatican wanted to do. When Ignatius was told about Carafa's election, he was thoroughly upset, and he went to the chapel to pray. Six minutes later, he emerged radiant and peaceful, certain that everything was in God's hands. (After Ignatius's death, Carafa did try to change the Society's structures, but he died before they could go into effect, and the next pope reversed the changes.)

When I first heard this story, I took it as one of those anecdotes people tell about saints that might be a bit of a tall tale—an incident that was buffed up and burnished in the telling to enhance the saint's credentials as a person of exceptional holiness. Could Ignatius have been *that* composed at the prospect of serious damage being done to the Jesuits, a work he was certain God wanted to continue? I didn't think so at the time, but I've changed my mind. That kind of detachment was certainly a quality Ignatius strived for. In fact, you might say that it's the very heart of the Spiritual Exercises. Ignatius's word for it was *indifference.*

What to Do about a Fabulous Fortune

Ignatius raises the issue of indifference and freedom in an exercise called the Three Classes of People, the third of four key meditations in the middle of the Exercises. The first of these is the Call of the King, in which we hear Christ call us to labor alongside him in his great work of healing the world. The second is the Two Standards, in which we learn that serving Christ involves taking on the virtues of poverty, obscurity, and humility. The Three Classes meditation invites us to examine our desires and attachments. More than any other exercise so far, it gets at what Ignatius said was the purpose of the Spiritual Exercises: "making ourselves ready to get rid of disordered affections." In the Three Classes exercise, we take a close look at what this really means.

The Three Classes exercise is a thought experiment. It puts people in an extreme situation and looks at how they would respond. Ignatius isn't moralizing, saying what we *should* do or labeling some behaviors good and others bad. Everyone in the exercise is trying to do the right thing. Think of them as people who've read the meditation on the Two Standards and taken to heart the message that riches can lead to ruin.

Here's the situation. These people have suddenly acquired a fortune of ten thousand ducats. A student at the University of Paris in Ignatius's time could live for a year on fifty ducats, so this is a fabulous fortune, beyond anyone's wildest dreams. It's like winning the Powerball lottery or having Google suddenly pay you a billion dollars for the rights to a computer program you've been tinkering with on your laptop. The people are thrilled; they look at the bags of gold and smile. But they are also serious Christians who understand that their attachment to this fortune can be a fearful distraction and temptation. They know what Paul wrote in the first letter to Timothy: "the love of money is the root of all evil." The problem isn't money per se. It's *love* of money. It's the disordered attachment.

The first class of people are all talk and no action. They talk about what to do—and they talk and talk for years. Finally, they die, attached to their fortune, never having done anything to free themselves from their love of it.

The second class of people are the negotiators and compromisers. They try to free themselves from the attachment by getting God to endorse their way of thinking. They pray that God will want what they want. They are like Jesus' would-be followers in Luke's Gospel who make excuses when Jesus calls them, who say, "Let me take care of some personal business first, and then I'll come."

People in the third class work to get free of the attachment to the money. They think seriously about giving it up. They act as if they weren't attached to the fortune even if they are. They resolve to do nothing about the fortune until they know what God wants. The only factor is "the desire to be better able to serve God our Lord."

What Are You Attached To?

Ignatius probably wrote this exercise between 1528 and 1535, during the seven years he spent at the University of Paris. He lived and worked with young men such as Peter Faber and Francis Xavier—smart, gifted, well-connected men who were getting an education at the finest university in the world to prepare for glamorous and well-compensated careers. The big prizes were bishoprics and other plum jobs in the church, which brought great wealth, power, and status. Think of Ignatius working today at Stanford University with grad students looking to get rich in Silicon Valley, or at Harvard with young people heading for riches on Wall Street.

Think about what this thought experiment might mean to you today. Ignatius dangled the lure of great wealth in front of the bright young men he lived with in Paris, and maybe you, too, are uneasy about your style of life and more-than-ample assets. Consider that the "fortune" in this exercise can be anything you're strongly attached to. You really, really want to get into an elite graduate school. You're in a relationship that feels good, sometimes very good, but some things about it trouble you, and it can't go on like this forever. Your life has changed—the kids are finally on their own, you don't need to work full-time, or you've retired—but you have a restless feeling that you are *too* comfortable and should do something new. The ten-thousand-ducat fortune can be anything that attracts you that's not sinful but that makes you uneasy. What do you do about it?

You can think about it for a while, maybe talk to some friends, but basically let it ride. Let events unfold in their own way. Go to Yale because that's what you've been longing for. Enjoy your relationship because you can't imagine living without him or her. Your business is booming; enjoy it. Take the kids to Disney World. This is how people in the first class handle the problem. Relax. Love God and do what you will. All will be well and all manner of things will be well. Remember, this is not wrong. The point of the exercise is to look at attachments, not to render judgments.

If letting it ride seems unsatisfactory, then you can bring God into the picture. Take the job, and pray that the extra money will be worth the extra work. Marry the boyfriend, and pray that all will be well. Thank God that Yale accepted you, and start praying for a good job when you're done so you can earn enough to pay off the student loans. This is the response of the people in the second class. They pursue the thing they long for, and then they ask God to come along for the ride. People in this second class may think that they are shaping their lives through their free choices, but in reality they are not free. They are controlled by their attachments.

The desired possessions, jobs, and relationships may be well worth having. In fact, we're assuming that everyone in this exercise is a righteous person, and that the success, honor, work, and companions they are pursuing are good things honestly acquired. But their choices are constrained because they leave God out of the decision-making process. People in the first class are afraid even to ask what God wants. Those in the second class simply assume that God wants what they want. Or if God doesn't, they pray that he will change his mind.

Those in the third class admit that they have a powerful attraction to the fortune, whatever it is, but they strive to detach themselves from it. They do something the others won't do: consider giving up the prize—giving the money away, turning down the job, refusing the honor, getting off the track they're on and doing something different. Put in Ignatian terms, they try to become indifferent. This doesn't mean they're uninterested; on the contrary, they *know* that they are attracted to the thing. It means that they work hard to make sure that this attraction doesn't influence a decision about what to do about it. They want only what God wants.

Let's be clear. The problem isn't the fortune; it's the *attraction* to the fortune. This exercise doesn't assume that God wants you to give the thing up. It may well be that God wants you to have it. But you need to have *freedom* to make a decision. The attitude we strive for is complete openness to whatever God wants. The attraction may not go away—in fact, we should assume that it won't. All our lives we will have many likes and dislikes, strong reactions to the things people do and don't do, passionate attraction to some possibilities and sharp revulsion to others. The challenge is to find a way to stand aside from these passions when important decisions are at hand so that we can perceive what God tells us is the best outcome.

It took Ignatius only six minutes to find peace when he learned that an enemy of the Jesuits had been elected pope. This doesn't mean that Ignatius came to think that Cardinal Carafa's election as pope was a good thing. It doesn't necessarily mean that his disappointment and anxiety went away entirely. But it does mean that he understood the course of events to be in God's hands, right where they belonged. If the new circumstances required Ignatius to make decisions, he would be able to decide wisely as long as his one desire was "to choose what is more for the glory of his Divine Majesty."

Stirring Things Up

You make the Spiritual Exercises because you're looking for something new. So here's a new idea: The key to choosing well is becoming free enough to know and choose what you really want. The conventional wisdom tells you to follow your bliss. Ignatius tells you to make sure that you're not entangled by those blissful passions. Make sure that your bliss is the real thing, that it represents you at your deepest level. The Three Classes exercise is just an exercise. It's intended to get you thinking, to suggest new ideas and to examine old ideas in a new light. Like the other exercises, it's a jumping-off point, a shift in perspective that changes the composition of the image and makes it look new. Here are a couple of things that the Three Classes helped me understand about attachments and desires.

For starters, the exercise's static "classes" schema isn't real. Reality is more complex. We can be in all three classes at any one time—ignoring a problem in one area, compromising in another, and achieving some degree of genuine freedom in yet another.

I remember the feeling of blessed release I felt when I stopped smoking. Getting free of nicotine was like getting out of jail. At the same time I was troubled about many things. I was praying that some plans I had would succeed, and I had quite deliberately decided not to look at some things that I knew were problems. Reality is dynamic; we are always gaining ground in some areas and losing it in others. So nobody falls completely into one category. The exercise describes three possible responses to attachments, all of which are in play right now, today.

The real subject of the exercise is desire. We desire many things. Some point us in the right direction; some don't. Some desires simplify things, and others make things more complicated. Some desires are strong; some are weak. We'd be better off if some of the strong desires were weaker and some weaker desires stronger. The Three Classes exercise compels us to think about what we desire and why.

Ask for What You Want

Ignatius loved desires. He was convinced that desire is the primary way God leads us to discover what we're meant to do—what will bring us joy and help us to serve his people. That's what happened to him when he was recovering from his injuries. He found the direction in life that would bring him the most joy by stimulating his desires and reflecting on what they meant. In the Spiritual Exercises he constantly instructs us, "Ask for what you want." There's a specific grace attached to each part of the Exercises, and we're to pray explicitly to receive this grace every time we sit down to pray through one of the exercises. Tell God what you want. Say it out loud. Get in touch with those "great desires" that are the fundamental forces that drive you.

This is a critical shift in attitude that we can experience through the Spiritual Exercises. We're accustomed to thinking about growth in virtue as a matter of curbing our appetites and desires, as if our appetites only drove us toward the dark side. Some do, but we also desire God and righteousness. Our deepest—truest—desires are for growth and change and for a fuller, deeper life. God actually speaks to us through such desires. These desires show us how to become the people God created us to be. We need to identify these desires, choose those that are of God, and follow them.

This is where the Three Classes exercise can help. It's a way to sort out the great desires from the disordered ones. Replace the ten-thousand-ducat fortune with the object of your desire and gauge the nature of your attachment to it. Can you imagine doing without it? Would you be devastated and heartsick if the desire is never satisfied? Are you free enough to walk away? Are you in touch with a desire deeper than the attachment to the thing you want, a desire to do only what God wants?

This kind of freedom isn't easy to achieve, but we shouldn't make it out to be harder than it is. Ignatian indifference doesn't mean that you stop wanting the thing you desire. Most of the time you won't, or can't, or shouldn't. But the practice of indifference will frustrate the power of wants and whims; they won't rule you anymore, which means that you'll be free to pursue what you truly want. You can attain this kind of freedom because it's a gift from God. Just ask for it.

Chapter 9

"It's Supposed to Be Hard"

The Three Kinds of Humility

One my favorite sports movies is *A League of Their Own,* which is about the All-American Girls Professional Baseball League, formed in the early 1940s when many male ballplayers had left the game to fight in World War II. Dottie Hinson is the star of the Rockford Peaches, and she frequently clashes with the manager, Jimmy Dugan, a former slugger with the Chicago Cubs whose career was cut short by his drinking. One day Dottie quits; she tells Jimmy she's going back home to get married. "Baseball just got too hard," she says. Jimmy looks her in the eye and says, "It's *supposed* to be hard. If it wasn't hard, everyone would do it. The hard . . . is what makes it great."

I reference Jimmy Dugan's pep talk because we probably need one right now as we work our way through the four major exercises of the second week. It's been getting harder. The Call of the King invited us to make an all-in, whole-hearted response to Christ's invitation to join him in his work. The Two Standards exercise challenges us to reject the most attractive features of Satan's program (wealth, honor, and glory) and embrace the least attractive features of Christ's (poverty, obscurity, and humility). Then the Three Classes exercise suggests that we must somehow get free of our natural attachments. It's like a trek up a mountain. The air gets thinner, the temperature drops, and the footing is more treacherous. It's getting harder.

Good, More Perfect, Most Perfect

The Three Kinds of Humility exercise takes our trek to a new level of difficulty. I thought of Dottie Hinson when I did this exercise. I felt like telling Dennis that the Spiritual Exercises just got too hard. But I didn't say that, because I knew he'd laugh and say something like what Jimmy Dugan said: the hard is what makes it great.

The Three Kinds of Humility exercise isn't a thought experiment or a scenario. There are no people in it and no imagery. It's straight propositional material—three kinds of humility, described in the abstract, set forth for our consideration. It's the last of four exercises leading up to what

Ignatius calls the Election, or choice. The Election could be a big decision—a choice of career, state of life, and the like—or it could be less monumental, such as a decision to rededicate yourself to the work you're already doing. Again, the point of the exercise isn't to find fault or to decree shoulds and shouldn'ts. All three kinds of humility are worthy. In fact, at any one time, you can probably see all three operating in you.

The first kind of humility is to conform oneself to God's law. This is no small task; living a righteous life means beating back temptations and struggling to do the right thing. But it's the least we can do. Ignatius doesn't think that the first kind of humility is an adequate basis for a wholehearted decision to join yourself with Christ in his work. If you want to be a disciple, you should want to do more than the minimum.

The second kind of humility is "more perfect than the first." This is the kind of freedom that Ignatius talked about in the Three Classes exercise. Ignatius repeats the words of the First Principle and Foundation. We don't prefer "riches rather than poverty, to seek honor rather than dishonor, to desire a long life rather than a short life." This is Ignatian indifference. You are drawn to all manner of things, but you don't let those attachments interfere with choosing the course that would serve Christ best.

Then there's the third kind of humility, which is called "the most perfect kind of humility." Instead of being detached from the things most people want, people with this third kind of humility positively desire the opposite. They *want* poverty, dishonor, and humiliation because they want to be with Jesus as fully as possible. They're able to say, "I desire to be accounted as worthless and a fool for Christ, rather than be esteemed as wise and prudent in this world." If we don't feel this way, Ignatius says, we're to pray that God will change our feelings so that we do. We're to ask God to choose us for a life marked by humiliation and insult, like Jesus' was.

See what I mean about the Spiritual Exercises getting too hard? The Three Kinds of Humility exercise is hard. It's hard to imagine how someone can function on a day-to-day basis with the mind-set of a person with the third kind of humility. To do your work well, you have to *want* it to succeed. You want people's respect, not their disdain. This brings up another problem. If you're doing work God has called you to do, doesn't wanting to be thought foolish and worthless mean that you're desiring God's work to fail? Worse still, insulting people and calling them fools is sinful behavior. Doesn't desiring these things amount to wanting other people to sin by calling you foolish?

The Worst Thing Imaginable

But wait—this is an *exercise*. Its purpose is to prepare you to make a decision about how to respond to Christ's invitation to work with him. The four exercises we've been examining emphasize certain graces and expose potential weaknesses. This isn't the way we're supposed to think all the time. In fact, Ignatius says that the three humilities exercise is something "to be thought over from time to time." Another point is that we're not to *seek* humiliation and poverty; rather, we're to *accept* them if they come. Ignatius always inserts a condition every time he mentions desiring something unappealing: we're to accept such hardship *provided that* God desires this for us.

Still, it's not easy to understand exactly what Ignatius was getting at here. I think this exercise can benefit from some cultural translation. Ignatius developed the Exercises while working with ambitious men preparing for careers in a society that especially valued status and honor. The coin of the realm in this world is what other people think of you, especially what powerful bishops, aristocrats, and potential patrons think of you. Academia is a modern culture that has some of these characteristics. I spent several years working as an editor in a large research university, and I was impressed by how sensitive academic people are to anything that affects their reputations. Who is publicly thanked, who is mentioned in the acknowledgments for a book, whose names go on a paper and in what order—all these things matter greatly in the academic world.

In such cultures, the worst thing imaginable is to be thought foolish and worthless. Ignatius had found his friends' weak spot, and he pushed on it. They might accept poverty. They might be ready to do difficult and disagreeable work. They might even welcome these things. But were they ready to choose a way of life that their patrons and families would think absurd and foolish? For these people, the test of the third kind of humility is a willingness to be despised. The Three Kinds of Humility exercise asks, are you humble enough to go forward with Christ in the face of the worst thing you can think of?

The worst thing for you may not be insults and dishonor. I know a guy who *welcomes* unpopularity. He cultivates an antiestablishment persona. He says he doesn't care what other people think about him. ("*That's* what you want other people to think about you," I say to myself). For him, the test of the third kind of humility might be a willingness to wear a suit and work in the public relations department of a large oil company, where he would spend his days burnishing the company's reputation. I know a woman, an entrepreneur, who is determined to call the shots. If she had a theme song, it would be Frank Sinatra's "My Way." She's started three businesses; she rarely takes vacations. She could probably work less and make more money if she took a conventional job, but she accepts the long hours and added stress as the price of the freedom she craves. For her, the test of the third kind of humility might be a willingness to give up her autonomy.

The Three Kinds of Humility exercise asks, "What are your nonnegotiables?" You say that your deepest desire is to follow Jesus wherever he may lead, but what limits do you put on how that will happen? Perhaps you see yourself as a leader, giving direction and setting the pace, or perhaps you see yourself as a follower, serving humbly on a team. Maybe you need to accomplish something noteworthy. Perhaps financial security comes first. Perhaps it's a certain style of service—a desk job, hands-on work, the life of the mind. The exercise asks you to look honestly at these deeply held ideas of the kind of person you are and what you need to have.

Remember that this is an exercise. Ignatius would be the last person to say that the best way to serve God is the one we find most unpleasant, difficult, and personally disagreeable. In fact, the truth is something like the opposite: God wants our life with him to fulfill our deepest desires for ourselves. He'll lead us to work for which we are suited. But the three humilities exercise asks us to examine our notion of what we're suited for. It's meant to stretch us, to open us up, to lead us to consider things that we think are off the table. And the exercise suggests that doing what we really want won't be a life of sweetness and light and perfect comfort. On the contrary, it means that we'll suffer. Hardship is involved, but the hard is what makes it great.

Why Should It Be Hard?

Let's ask a basic—and somewhat unnerving—question. Why should hardship and suffering have anything to do with following Christ? We're accustomed to this idea because Christianity embedded it in Western culture. Gordon Gekko ("Greed is good") and Vince Lombardi ("winning is the only thing") might be modern-day heroes, but we still admire people who renounce it all. The best stories are about people who prevail through suffering. Three of the top five most admired people of the twentieth century are Mother Teresa, Martin Luther King, and Helen Keller—people whose great accomplishments were rooted in great hardship. We need to step back and see how radical this idea is. The Sermon on the Mount is often regarded as the epitome of Jesus' moral teaching, but notice how little worldly sense it makes. Lowly peasants are going to inherit the earth? We're supposed to love our enemies? Bless our persecutors? Give our possessions to people who are stealing from us?

Friedrich Nietzsche, of all people, helped me see how radical the gospel is. I studied a lot of philosophy in college (it was a Jesuit institution), and Nietzsche got my attention because he was a passionate iconoclast who wrote well. He rejected Christianity, but he didn't pay lip service to generosity, kindness, and humility, as most nonbelievers do. Nietzsche rejected *all* of it. He called Christian virtue a "slave morality," a moral code developed by oppressed people in reaction to their oppressors. The Jews and early Christians couldn't overthrow their hated oppressors, so instead they rejected everything they stood for, especially their moral code. The Romans lived by a code of power, glory, and strength, so the Christians valued humility, weakness, and suffering. This is a fascinating theory, but a simplistic one. Nietzsche couldn't imagine a kind of humility embraced in the imitation of Christ, whose greatness sprang from his lowliness. Still, Nietzsche's unsentimental gaze underlines how strange the gospel is. The cross is shocking. The Sermon on the Mount rejects the values of the world. When Ignatius suggests that we desire to be thought "worthless and a fool for Christ," he's touching the very heart of who Christ is.

Art often expresses such truths better than theology and philosophy do—at least that's the case for me. I grasped something about what the humility of Christ means when I read the novel *The Samurai* by the Japanese Catholic Shusaku Endo. The story is about a group of Japanese merchants and nobles of the seventeenth century who travel to the Americas and Europe with a group of Spanish Catholics. The samurai of the title is a bit like Nietzsche in that he looks at Christianity through the eyes of a nonbeliever and is surprised by what he sees. But unlike Nietzsche, he grasps the essential nature of Christ, and it's not the grand triumphant Christ of the Spanish Empire and papal splendor in Rome. Instead, it's the crucified Christ, "that ugly, emaciated figure with his arms and legs nailed to a cross, and his head dangling limply down." The samurai understands why he sees "a pathetic statue of that man" in every home he visits on his travels:

> Somewhere in the hearts of men there's a yearning for
> someone who will be with you throughout your life, some-
> one who will never betray you, never leave you—even if
> that someone is a sick, mangy dog. That man became just
> such a miserable dog for the sake of mankind.

The samurai becomes a Christian. Reflecting on Christ's
words, "greater love hath no man than this, that he lay
down his life for his friends," he returns to Japan, where he
is martyred, in humble imitation of his Master.

The mysterious secret of this kind of humility is that the
greatest love and, ultimately, the greatest deeds, aren't possible without it. Great virtue is born of great suffering. We
don't know how much we need Christ until we need him
desperately. We don't know how much Christ can do until
we badly need him to do something. We don't know how
good we can be until we need to be better than we are. The
greatest misfortune imaginable to Ignatius's friends at the
University of Paris was to fall into poverty and to be thought
foolish and worthless. For us it could be something else: a
crippling illness, disappointment in love, a lost job, a failed
career, a fractured family, a broken marriage, the disabili-
ties of aging, a grinding and tedious struggle to make ends
meet and care for people whom you sometimes feel aren't
doing enough to care for themselves. Misfortune comes to

all of us, and when it does, we will find Jesus there too. We will find that Jesus gives us the strength to do what seems impossible—and above all to bring new life out of misfortune. This is the paschal mystery lived out.

My wife and I volunteer for an association of parents who have children with Down syndrome. We hear the same story over and over: a child whose arrival appeared to be a terrible misfortune turns out to be the bearer of grace. Parents show generosity, courage, and creativity they didn't know they had. In fact, they *didn't* have these qualities until their disabled child came into their lives. We all know people like these parents of children with Down syndrome: people who become better people because misfortune, trouble, and suffering come their way. That's why the best stories are about people who overcome adversity. That's why Mother Teresa, Martin Luther King, and Helen Keller were the people they were, and that's why we admire them.

But we've also seen the opposite: people who fall apart when tragedy strikes, people who run away, people who retreat into themselves, people who complain and grow bitter. We have a choice. The Three Kinds of Humility exercise emphasizes what it means to follow Christ. It's the time when we say, "When suffering comes, and it *will* come, I want it to make me more like Christ."

The Miracle of Empty Hands

Another novel helped me understand what true humility can make possible. It's *The Diary of a Country Priest* by Georges Bernanos, a novel presented in the form of a diary kept by a young, frail, naive, and not-terribly-gifted priest struggling to get a pastoral ministry going in a rural French village. Outwardly, he's a pathetic figure, mocked by children, ignored and patronized by adults, and rebuffed by his superiors. He thinks he's a miserable failure. He struggles to pray. His health is failing. He's the exemplar of the third kind of humility because he is thought to be worthless and a fool. He thinks so himself. And yet his simplicity and honesty have an extraordinary impact. Everyone senses his straightforward, sincere love; some eventually respond in kind. The haughty local count tells him, "Your simplicity is a kind of flame which scorches them. You go through the world with that lowly smile of yours as though you begged the world their pardon for being alive, while all the time you carry a torch."

The priest (who is never named in the novel) ministers to the local countess, a tormented woman who has shut herself off from God and lived in bitterness for many years. His simple love and humble truth-telling break through to her hard heart, and she finds peace. The priest writes in his diary, "O miracle—thus to be able to give what we ourselves do not possess, sweet miracle of our empty hands! Hope which was shriveling in my heart flowered again in hers; the spirit of prayer which I thought lost in me forever was given back to her by God."

The early Christians sang a hymn that was incorporated into Paul's description of Christ in Philippians 2:6–8:

> Who, though he was in the form of God,
> > did not regard equality with God
> > as something to be exploited,
> but emptied himself,
> > taking the form of a slave,
> > being born in human likeness.
> And being found in human form,
> > he humbled himself
> > and became obedient to the point of death—
> > even death on a cross.

Paul continues.

> *Therefore* God also highly exalted him
> > and gave him the name
> > that is above every name,
> so that at the name of Jesus
> > every knee should bend,
> > in heaven and on earth and under the earth,

and every tongue should confess
    that Jesus Christ is Lord,
    to the glory of God the Father.

—Philippians 2:9–11, italics added

This third kind of humility—the miracle of empty hands—is about what humility allows us to do. Christ's lowliness made him master of creation. The country priest's humility allowed the people of his village to experience God's love. Humility allows God to use us to do God's work for the salvation of the world.

A fulfilling life entails lots of hard work. For many of us it means getting an education, finding a spouse, and raising a family. For all of us it means false starts, failures, disappointments, and long hours of tedious labor. It means taking care of others and doing what they want instead of what you want. A fulfilling life means that you will never do some things you want to do. But this is how you become the person you were meant to be. As you lose your false self, you find your true self.

Chapter 10

What Are You Feeling?

Discerning the Spirits

I have a friend, whom I'll call Bruce, who made a steady living for years as the owner of the local franchise of a national retail chain. One day the parent company suddenly bought him out. The company was being sold, and it needed to own all its franchises. Suddenly, Bruce was a millionaire. A windfall is something unearned—it's the fruit that's blown out of the trees and onto the ground, free for the taking. Bruce's good fortune was a classic windfall, but unfortunately, he interpreted the event as evidence that he was a pretty smart businessman, smarter than anyone thought (including himself). He then proceeded to make several unwise investments. He launched a couple of start-ups, but they failed. He lost most of his money. Bruce didn't often ask other people's opinions about his business ideas, and he liked to "go with his gut" when making decisions instead of laboriously analyzing business plans and budgets. Unfortunately, his gut was wrong most of the time.

Bruce was led astray by his feelings; his euphoria about his money led him to inaccurate conclusions about his abilities. I'll bet Bruce's business mentality after the buyout was similar to the attitude of a foolish gambler who has just won four or five hands in a row at the blackjack table: "Winning that much must mean I'm pretty smart about cards. Let's do that again." But blackjack is a game of chance with the odds in favor of the house, and thinking that you'll keep winning at blackjack is pretty dumb.

If Ignatius knew Bruce (and I'm sure he knew people like him), he'd probably say that his decisions showed a lack of proper discernment. Ignatius knew a lot about discernment. In fact, his twenty-two "rules for discernment" are unmatched for their insight and clarity. Discernment of spirits is a topic very much in vogue these days, and most of what's said about it is an elaboration on what Ignatius wrote five hundred years ago. We can use the rules for discernment quite often—every day, in fact.

An Art and a Science

Discernment is good judgment, wisdom, and the ability to distinguish between the sound and the unsound, the true and the false, the good and the bad—and also the better from the merely good. It's the wisdom that enables us to distinguish feelings, ideas, and motives that are from the Holy Spirit from those that aren't. It shows us the choices that lead to God and those that don't.

Ignatius believed that discernment involves both an inner sense and objective criteria—it's both an art and a science. The art part of it—the spiritual sense—is something we get better at as we grow in spiritual maturity and sensitivity. Certainly in the Ignatian view this would involve making the Spiritual Exercises, praying the daily examen, and cultivating a habit of reflective awareness of the presence of God and of other spirits. With experience, we become better able to discern the spirits and interpret what they mean. But discernment also operates according to certain principles. This is the science part of discernment, and that's what I aim to explain in this chapter.

Ignatius's rules for discernment come in two sets. The first is a basic set that explains what the spirits are and how they operate. The second set of rules gets into more nuanced and hard-to-discern situations. *Advanced* isn't quite the right word to describe the second set because these rules are quite useful for anyone who has been making any kind of a sustained effort to have a fruitful spiritual life, which I hope includes everyone who's gotten this far in this book. Ignatius drew on Christian tradition when he wrote the rules, but his main source of insight was years of careful and Spirit-guided observation of the workings of spirits in the lives of real-life people of all personalities, temperaments, and inclinations. The rules are not theories. They describe how spirits actually work.

How Real Are Evil Spirits?

What (or who) are these spirits? I think we can all agree that good spirits are present in our lives. The Holy Spirit of God is active in the world; what's more, the Holy Spirit is a Person—a personality and a presence. Evil spirits are more controversial. Ignatius (and most Christians through-out history) thought that evil spirits were persons and presences as well—as real as the Holy Spirit. For Ignatius, the image in the Two Standards exercise of two oppos-ing armies, Christ's and Satan's, was more than just a metaphor.

Today, many people question the notion of personal evil spirits who "prowl about the world seeking the ruin of souls," as an old Catholic prayer puts it. They prefer to see Satan as a personification of all that's in us that opposes the good. Fair enough, but I'm mindful of one of C. S. Lewis's most acute observations in *Mere Christianity*—that Satan's strategy to disguise his presence leads some people to see devils everywhere and leads others to disbelieve in him entirely. Call it what you will—evil spirits, Satan, the devil, the enemy, or the dark side. There are spiritual forces at work that drag us down and wish us ill. Ignatius called the evil spirit "the enemy of our human nature." That's a helpful way to think about it. The good spirit has us on the road to freedom. The bad spirit wants to drive us into the ditch.

Spirits are in ceaseless conflict within us and in the world. Sometimes it's mild pushing and shoving. Sometimes it's a fierce tug-of-war. Sometimes it's a pitched battle, with hand-to-hand combat following an artillery barrage. Spiritual forces that move us toward God contend with those that move us away from him. Part of us wants to do the right thing; part of us doesn't. This spiritual struggle throws up a maelstrom of feelings, thoughts, and impulses, and these are the raw material for discernment.

Consolation and Desolation

The first thing Ignatius did to sort through this confusion was to name the two main clusters of feelings: *consolation* and *desolation*. These are odd, somewhat old-fashioned words for feelings that are quite commonplace. *Consolation* refers to feeling connected to God, a conviction that things are OK, that you're headed in the right direction. *Desolation* is the gnawing sense that things are wrong, especially that something's wrong with *you*. Consolation usually feels like gentleness and assurance. Desolation usually feels like anxiety, discomfort, and sadness. Consolation points outward, toward God and others. Desolation turns you inward, away from God and others, toward yourself and all the things that are bothering you.

Consolation and desolation aren't the same as feeling good and feeling bad. They are *spiritual* states; they're about moving toward or away from God, It's not necessarily desolation to be disappointed when you don't get the promotion you've been hoping for. It might well be desolation if you think not getting the promotion means that you're incompetent or that your bosses are out to get you. We often experience consolation as confidence and hope in the midst of hard times. You might not feel very cheerful when you tackle a difficult work or family problem, but the assurance you feel as you do so means that you're in a state of consolation.

Consolation and desolation are textures of everyday life. They run through our moods. They influence our dealings with people, our choices, and our reactions to events and circumstances. The first step in discernment is to identify which state has the upper hand.

It All Depends

A basic principle of discernment—and one of the most important—is that good spirits and evil spirits operate differently according to our spiritual condition. Consequently, feelings of consolation and desolation can mean different things. Right off the bat we discover that discernment is no simple matter.

For someone who is already on a harmful course, the evil spirit will stir up emotions that feel like consolation. Sin will look good—satisfying, pleasurable, richly justified—because the wily bad spirit doesn't want anything to change. The good spirit will try to make such a person discontented and unhappy, hoping that this will motivate the person to change course. The reverse is true for a spiritually maturing person. The good spirit will reinforce good choices with consolation, and the evil spirit will throw sand in the works in the form of anxiety, sadness, and doubts.

Real life is dynamic; we're usually spiritually strong and spiritually weak at the same time. I know a guy who is a beloved mentor and colleague at work and a mercurial tyrant at home. He feels bad about the way he treats his kids (desolation from the good spirit), and he feels neglected and ineffective at work (desolation from the evil spirit). At other times he feels that his angry confrontation with his son was justified (consolation from the evil spirit) and that God has blessed him with good work and good colleagues (consolation from the good spirit). You can see how quickly discernment becomes complicated. It's a subtle art, best practiced with the assistance of a spiritual director who can help you identify the nuances.

When You're Feeling Low—Be Patient

Ignatius's basic rules for discernment are mostly concerned with handling desolation. That fact in itself tells us a lot; desolation is a common, routine experience. You will frequently feel bored, dissatisfied, anxious, and harassed by the feeling that things aren't right. These feelings are normal. Of course, desolation doesn't *feel* normal—it feels *abnormal*. When you're upset, you think that something's gone wrong and that you need to do something to set things right. Most of the time, that's exactly what you shouldn't do. The first rule for handling desolation is to make no important changes in your life. Ignatius said, "We should never make any change, but remain firm and constant in the resolution and decision which guided us the day before the desolation."

That sounds like common sense, but common sense is often the first casualty of a serious bout with desolation. When you're feeling low, you want to do *something* to make the bad feelings go away. Quit the job. Move away. Teach the kid a lesson. Dump the girlfriend or boyfriend (or, if you're the one who got dumped, find another one as quickly as possible).

Sometimes a change is needed, but desolation is the worst possible time to figure out what it should be. Wait until the emotional storms pass—and the storms *will* pass—and *then* decide whether anything needs to change. This is another of Ignatius's rules: be patient. Wait upon the Lord. Peace and tranquility will return. This is another commonsensical point we need to be reminded of, because one of the nastiest features of desolation is the feeling that it will last forever, or at least for a very long time. It won't. Desolation ceases to be so desolate when we're reminded that it will soon pass.

Our emotional lives are cyclical affairs. Anxiety and contentment, joy and sorrow, peace and turmoil—all these come and go. These feelings are produced by the ceaseless, deep-down spiritual struggle in our divided hearts, much of which takes place beyond our consciousness. Ignatius encourages us not to be upended by this. Sit tight and wait for the feelings to change.

Patience is just the first step. Desolation is an opportunity for spiritual growth and progress. When in desolation, rouse yourself, Ignatius says. Pray more than usual. Do good works for others. Don't sit passively by as the evil spirit messes with your mind. Launch a counterattack. It's good advice, and another example of Ignatius's psychological insight, because lethargy is a common feature of desolation. Often, desolation *is* lethargy. Ignatius advises us to face it head-on. When you don't want to pray, pray more. When you feel like isolating yourself, spend as much time with other people as possible.

When You're Feeling Great—Be Careful

We need Ignatius's first set of rules for discernment because desolation is a common experience. We need his second set because of another unwelcome fact: consolation isn't always what it seems. Sometimes it's *false* consolation that the evil spirit uses to deceive us. False consolation can blind us to things that need to change; it can lead us to make bad decisions. That's so, writes Ignatius, because "it is a mark of the evil spirit to appear as an angel of light."

This shouldn't be surprising. The enemy of our human nature isn't stupid. If you've been sincerely trying to lead a virtuous life for a while, you're not likely to give in to a temptation to do something blatantly wrong. To throw you off track, the evil spirit disguises things. You'll find credible explanations for bad behavior ("I was tired," "That's the way she is," "He had to get it out of his system"). You'll find plausible excuses for dangerous complacency ("I need a break," "I can handle this," "I'll get to that some other time"). You'll find reasons to keep silent when you should speak up, and reasons to intervene when you shouldn't. You might make bad decisions because you're excited about something you want to do or possess, and you think the excitement comes from God.

Ignatius puts it this way: "It is characteristic of the evil one to fight against [true] happiness and consolation by proposing fallacious reasonings, subtleties, and continual deceptions." The evil spirit produces *false* consolations, not the real thing. The devil may be smart, but he's wicked, too. He doesn't have the capacity to give us genuine consolation—only God can do that. Counterfeit money is never perfect; a close look can always find the forgery. The second set of rules for discernment is about exposing counterfeit consolation for what it is.

Ignatius tells us that consolation comes in two forms: with a cause and without one. Sometimes consolation just happens. For no apparent reason, our hearts are flooded with a joyful peace, or we suddenly feel intense gratitude for what God has given us. This happened to me one day when I was driving alone in a rental car on the New Jersey Turnpike toward Newark airport. Suddenly, I was seized by the conviction that God loved me—me, personally, Jim. Everyone I know has had experiences like this. The feeling of joy comes unexpectedly, for no good reason, and it's often quite the opposite of what you'd expect in the circumstances. Ignatius calls this kind of experience "consolation without preceding cause." Such consolation is always from God. We can enjoy these moments, confident that the bad spirit won't be using them to lead us astray.

It's the other kind of consolation that we have to worry about; Ignatius calls it "consolation with preceding cause." If you know why you are feeling energized or peaceful or happy or otherwise consoled—or if you have a good idea why—then you should take a close look at where the feeling comes from and examine what it means. The evil spirit might be involved.

I'm struck by the way this principle, like many other Ignatian guidelines and "rules," reverses the way I usually think about things. I'm suspicious of consolation without cause and credulous about consolation that I think I understand. I didn't get very excited about my epiphany on the New Jersey Turnpike. I chalked it up to fatigue, the exhilaration of travel, or the thrill of being back in the state where I grew up. I didn't really do what Ignatius said I should do about this kind of consolation—namely, enjoy it and thank God for it. By contrast, I tend to accept consolation with cause easily, and that can be a mistake. Say I'm feeling good because someone wants to hire me for a freelance writing project. I might go right ahead and accept that job ("Hey, someone recognizes my talent, and they're going to give me *money*!"), not asking what price I'll pay in time and energy, or considering the strain it might put on my other commitments.

Questions to Ask about Consolation

Ignatius advises that we discern the spirits in the middle and at the end of a new venture, not just at the beginning. Something that begins well can end in sorrow. The enemy is a wily deceiver. "He begins by suggesting thoughts that are suited to a devout soul, and ends by suggesting his own," Ignatius writes. This is the plot of Shakespeare's *Othello*: the wicked Iago flatters Othello to gain his trust so that he can destroy him. Tolstoy depicts the same thing in *Anna Karenina*: Anna's road to disgrace and death begins with her delighted response to a man's generosity and flattery. Several years ago, a man I know began to be concerned about the food he was eating; today, he is neurotically obsessed with his diet and consumed by fears about processed food and environmental toxins. I have many friends who have burned themselves out doing good works. We need to be alert to peace and confidence turning into what Ignatius calls "disturbance of the soul."

Another of Ignatius's principles is that the "feeling" of the consolation is an important indicator of its source. Genuine consolation is usually gentle and welcoming. Ignatius says it's like a drop of water hitting a sponge; it's like walking through an open door into your own house. False consolation is noisy and disturbing, like someone banging on a locked door. This principle might have helped my friend Bruce, the windfall millionaire. He was elated when he got rich, but it was a noisy elation. Full of restless energy, Bruce rushed forward with grand but flawed plans.

One final rule: beware of the "afterglow" of a consolation from God. It's entirely possible to receive a consolation from God and then go on to make a bad decision. Don't be like my friend Ben, who had a profound spiritual experience while on a pilgrimage to the Franciscan shrines in Assisi. Ben thought that God wanted him to change his life completely to imitate Francis. He thought he should quit his job, drop out of an MBA program, and move his young family to a poor neighborhood so they could minister to the homeless. (Ben changed his mind when he got home from Italy and talked to his wife.)

Discernment as a Way of Life

I kept a journal while making the Spiritual Exercises and read through it months after the Exercises ended. My early notes had a lot to do with ideas and questions, such as "What's the real point of the story of Abraham and Isaac?" and "How should I think about hell?" Over time, the focus shifted to feelings, intuitions, impressions, and other non-cognitive ways of knowing. There are notes about my moods (often dark) and about what I felt when I prayed (a lot about gratitude). Gradually, I let my emotions take the lead, and they led me to the most rewarding reflections I had during the Exercises. This habit has stuck with me.

People ask, "How did the Spiritual Exercises change you?" One of the biggest differences is that now I pay attention to the "affective" part of myself that's hard to put into words. I've learned that my feelings are often God whispering in my ear, "Look here. Something important is going on. Understand what this means."

We can use the rules for discernment every day. We can make discernment a way of life. We're regularly perplexed by events and circumstances. We often find ourselves slogging through times of anxiety and gloom. We frequently feel pretty good—and wonder whether the glow is a gift from God or an invitation to feel smug and complacent.

Ignatian discernment is helpful for those little decisions that come up all the time: "Do I back off this problem or push harder on it? When am I going to make that phone call I've been avoiding? Should I continue to read this book? Do I need to pay closer attention to what my wife is saying? Am I wasting my time?" These small decisions are much easier to make when we approach them with a discerning awareness of the ebb and flow of spiritual feelings.

Discernment is good for the big decisions, too. Some we make only once—to get married, for example. But other kinds of significant choices come up more often. Next, we'll look at the Ignatian approach to making decisions.

Chapter 11

It Seemed Like a Good Idea at the Time

Making Decisions

Some years ago, my wife and I sold our home in Ann Arbor and moved to a city in Indiana, which shall remain name-less because it isn't to blame for the miserable time we had there. The move split up our family; one child came with us while two others stayed in Michigan. We bought a house that didn't suit us well. We lived in an isolated neighbor-hood where we felt like strangers. Everything seemed a bit off, and soon we compounded the problem by feeling sorry for ourselves and longing for the people and places we left behind. A year later, we moved back to Ann Arbor and bought a house three blocks away from our old one. The whole episode was an expensive, painful mistake.

We could have foreseen every problem we had in Indiana, but we didn't. I don't recall that my wife and I ever sat down and considered the cons as well as the pros. We were excited—a new place, new experiences, and a new job. All the signs pointed toward making the move. We looked confidently at the exciting future and ignored the dark lining in the silver cloud. Moving to Indiana seemed like a good idea at the time. Napoleon's invasion of Russia, Prohibition, the introduction of "New" Coke, and every other disastrous decision you can think of—they all seemed like good ideas at the time.

That's because we human beings are highly irrational when it comes to making decisions. Cognitive scientists who have studied decision making have compiled a long list of "cognitive biases" that practically guarantee that any decision that works out well does so by accident. Here are a few of them. When it's decision time, most people have a good idea of what they want to do, and they will systematically look for reasons to do it and ignore reasons not to. (My wife and I did exactly that.) When facing a family or work problem, we tend to overestimate the amount of control we have over the situation. In weighing future events, the most recent thing that happened (the stock is up 10 percent this month!) has more impact on us than more distant events (the stock is still down for the year). We prefer small immediate benefits to greater long-term benefits. We underestimate the time it will take to finish a job. We overestimate our ability to resist temptation and to show restraint when provoked. We'll see patterns in past events where none actually exist. When good things happen, we think we're responsible. When things turn sour, it's not our fault. We think that attractive people are smarter and nicer than people with crooked noses, sagging jowls, and thinning hair.

If you're like me, you'll laugh at all this and think, "Not *me*. I'm the exception. Cognitive biases are generalizations based on data plotted on a bell curve. I'm over there on the edge, with the smart people. *I* am not so easily misled." If that's what you think, you have lots of company. Most people think they're smarter, more accurate, luckier, and more objective than everybody else. Everybody lives in Garrison Keillor's Lake Wobegon, where all the children are above average, and all the adults are, too.

Decisions Are Limited

Ignatius knew nothing of cognitive science, but he knew people, and he probably observed all of these cognitive biases in action. He probably observed at least some of them at work in himself as well. One of the more remarkable (and reassuring) aspects of Ignatius's story is the large number of decisions he made that didn't work out as he planned. He went to the Holy Land, thinking that God wanted him to live there; the authorities put him on the first ship back to Europe. He thought he should fast strenuously, punish his body, and practice other severe penances; this turned out to be a bad mistake. He thought the Jesuits should own very little property; in his lifetime they were running an international network of schools and other institutions, becoming champion fund-raisers and smart money managers in the process. He thought God wanted him to be an itinerant teacher, preacher, and evangelist; he spent the last fourteen years of his life in Rome, running the Jesuits from a small suite of offices. Twice he refused the office of superior general after his brother Jesuits elected him. His confessor had to practically order him to change his mind.

So it's with some irony that we celebrate Ignatius as the master of discernment and decision making. He knew very well that he was working with fallible, easily misled human beings who didn't know how fallible they were. That's why he developed the Spiritual Exercises. They came into existence as Ignatius worked with people making decisions about what they were going to do with their lives. The evil spirit knows all about those cognitive biases. That's why Ignatius brought heavy spiritual artillery to bear on the problem of decision making.

Before we look at what Ignatius said, it's a good idea to understand the limits of the Ignatian approach to decision making. The most that Ignatian discernment can promise is that you can have some reasonable assurance about what God wants for *you* in *your* particular circumstances. It doesn't give knowledge of the future, and it doesn't guarantee that the project or job change or marriage will be a success. It doesn't even promise that the thing will happen. You and your spouse might decide, after much prayer and discernment, that God wants you to adopt a child, but the adoption might fall through for any number of reasons. You might decide that God wants you to be married, but you may never find someone right for you who wants to marry you. My wife and I might have moved to Indiana after a careful discernment and still have had a bad time of it there.

That's because other people are free—as you are. Your discernment has to do with *you* and no one else. Your decision doesn't indicate what other people should do or will do. Neither can you say that someone who takes a view contrary to yours is opposing God's will.

Ignatius displayed this remarkably humble attitude in 1552 when he resisted Pope Julius III's plans to make another Jesuit a cardinal. Ignatius detested the idea; Jesuits were committed to poverty, and the office of cardinal at the time brought with it wealth and a luxurious life. Ignatius lobbied hard to scuttle the idea, writing, "If I did not act thus, I would be quite certain that I would not give a good account of myself before God Our Lord." But he went on to say that others were free to disagree with him: "The same Spirit could inspire me to take one point of view for some reasons and inspire others to the contrary for other reasons." (The pope eventually changed his mind.)

Think about that. Ignatius thought it was OK for people to disagree with him about a matter he thought was important. In fact, God could be moving each party in a dispute to hold the views they had. Ignatius could be wrong (although he thought he was right). God could be allowing this clash of views for some larger purpose. Imagine what debate in the church would be like if people held their views as humbly as Ignatius did. Imagine if our politics were conducted this way.

The Decision Isn't the Most Important Thing

At this point you might ask, why bother? Why should you spend time and effort on discerning decisions if you can't know that the choice will have a good outcome, or even that the plan you are considering will happen at all? We bother with discernment because, in the Ignatian perspective, the decision isn't the most important thing. It's the means, not the end. The end is to live a life that pleases God and satisfies our deepest longings. The choices we make serve this end; they're of secondary importance.

So the first principle of Ignatian decision making is to *seek God first.* The end for which we were created is to "praise, reverence, and serve God our Lord," as the First Principle and Foundation puts it. The "things on the face of the earth"—jobs, people, money, knowledge, art, science, everything—are there to help us achieve this end.

Much of the time we have it backward. We make the decision first (employing all our wishful thinking, selective memory, and other cognitive biases) and then ask God to bless it. You might decide to marry your boyfriend, and then turn the marriage over to God, praying that it will be successful. You might decide to take that attractive new job, and pray that it will turn out as well as you hope. My wife and I prayed that our move to Indiana would go well—*after* we decided to move. Many of the exercises in the Spiritual Exercises are designed to help us get our priorities straight. The important thing is to walk with Christ. You don't make decisions to please yourself, advance your interests, or meet your goals. It's not about you.

Instead, it's about a life with God, and this journey may well be a meandering one. The outcome of your decisions is contingent on a host of factors out of your control, especially the decisions of other people. Decisions lead to more decisions. If plan A doesn't work out, there's always plan B—and plans C, D, E, and F. Even important decisions that turn out to be serious mistakes can be redeemed. Ignatian decision making isn't linear. It's more like a spiral—a process of reflection, choice, further reflection, and more choices that carries us deeper into a life lived more and more for God.

The second principle of making sound choices is to *know what you truly desire*. "Put God first" and "find out what you truly want" are really two ways of talking about the same thing. "God's will" isn't a blueprint. It's more like a vision for the kind of person you can become in the particular set of circumstances in which you find yourself. God has planted this vision in your heart; it's what you truly desire. In that perspective, God's desires and our deepest desires are the same thing. The problem, as we've seen, is that we're attached to all sorts of things that obscure our deepest desires. We want money and acclaim. We're in thrall to a certain idea of the good life. We're wedded to the social roles we play—the peacemaker, the rebel, the parent, the know-it-all. The Three Classes of People and the Three Kinds of Humility exercises draw our attention to these disordered attachments and challenge us to get free of them.

Ignatius's third principle of sound decision making is to learn to *trust and understand your feelings and other noncognitive ways of knowing.* At first glance this might seem surprising, even dangerous. Feelings are subjective. The cognitive biases that lead our decision making astray involve powerful feelings. How can we trust them? Wouldn't we be better off distancing ourselves from emotions and trying to place our decision making on a solid rational footing? Ignatius thought not. He thought that discernment of feelings was the key to making a good decision.

Recall the story of Ignatius's conversion. He daydreamed about the stories he read while lying around waiting for his legs to heal. Stories about Jesus and the saints left him feeling happy; stories of romance and derring-do left him listless and depressed. He realized that God was using these feelings to point him toward the future that would bring him the most joy. Desolation told him that a career at the court of Seville was a dead end. Consolation told him that his deepest desire was to be like Christ. His feelings took him to a place where his reason couldn't go.

Yes, our feelings can be unruly and misleading, but that's what the rules for discernment of spirits are for—to show us when feelings are leading us to God and when they're not. Ignatius believed that discernment of spirits should be part of any good process of decision making. In the end, we should know with a high degree of certitude which choice is the right one, and the sign of this is a feeling of consolation that comes from God.

Three Ways to Make a Decision

With these principles in place—seek God first, know what you really want, and understand your feelings—you can set out to make a good decision. Ignatius doesn't think you should be doing this alone if the decision is an important one. He assumes that you'll have the help of a spiritual director or another wise counselor. This is good practical advice; spiritual directors broaden the perspective, picking up things that we miss and spotting those pesky cognitive biases. Bringing someone else into the picture is also a wise spiritual principle; Ignatius thought that a desire to keep things secret was a sure sign of the work of the evil spirit.

If you're reluctant to talk to someone else about a decision you're facing, ask yourself why.

Sometimes the job is finished almost as soon as it begins: God lets us know the right choice with complete clarity. Sometimes the circumstances are dramatic; Paul is stricken with a vision of Christ on the road to Damascus. Sometimes they're ordinary. In the novel *Anna Karenina*, a character suddenly understands the truth about his life when he overhears a peasant's offhand remark. Ignatius calls this "first time election." It's a revelation that we don't doubt is from God. The sudden, lightning-bolt, no-doubt-about-it decision happens infrequently. God seems to prefer to work through the ordinary processes of life. But God can intervene directly, and sometimes he does.

More often, we'll experience strong, conflicting emotions as we consider two or more positive, plausible courses of action. Should I get a master's degree? Start my own business? Retire? Move to Indiana? You think, *Yes, I'll do that,* and an assortment of feelings will surface: excitement, dread, joy, and fear. You think, *No, I won't do that,* and you feel a different configuration of emotions. We use the principles of Ignatian discernment to determine the source of the feelings of consolation and desolation. Is that anxious feeling desolation from the evil spirit, who is trying to deflect you from the right path, or is it the good spirit tugging on your shirttail telling you to beware? Or perhaps it's just normal anxiety without any particular spiritual significance.

To evaluate alternatives, Ignatius suggests that you use your imagination. Imagine that you've chosen one of the alternatives—you're in school, you've started the business, you've retired. Now imagine your new life as vividly as you can. What is your day like? What kind of problems do you run into? What do you like most? What do you like least? Now imagine having taken the other path—you'll keep working instead of retiring, you'll keep your day job instead of starting a business. How does *that* feel? Feel the feelings generated by these scenarios, and discern their spiritual meaning. Ignatius suggests another imaginative exercise: Imagine that a close friend is facing the same decision and has come to talk it over with you. Listen to your friend speak. What does your friend emphasize? What does he or she skip over? Observe your friend's body language. When your friend asks for advice, what do you say?

Ignatius called this mode of discernment the "second time election." He thought it was the usual way people make a decision—especially an important one.

Finally, there's the "third time election"—the mode of decision making we use when we don't have particularly strong feelings about the alternatives. Ignatius preferred discernment of the second kind, in which emotions point to the activity of the good and bad spirits. But it sometimes happens that feelings aren't burning hotly at decision time. In these cases we analyze the options, weigh the pros and cons, and otherwise bring our minds to bear on the situation.

No matter how a decision gets made—in the first, second, or third modes—it needs to be confirmed. Often we neglect this step or skip it entirely. A tentative decision can morph into a final one without your noticing. Here we run into the problem that cognitive scientists call confirmation bias—our tendency to look for reasons to do what we're inclined to do. It's a special danger here at the end. You've made the decision; you're strongly inclined to make it final, saying something like, "I feel peaceful about this." Not so fast. Ignatius says we should turn "with great diligence to prayer" and ask God to confirm the decision.

Decisions in Real Life

By now you might be saying something like, "That's fine, but how often does it really work out that way?" I've edited dozens of books that purport to give practical spiritual advice (I've also written a few), and I always wonder how well the theory holds up when people apply it to their lives. A couple of years ago, I watched a video of a crazy play at the end of a college football game. Time ran out as the ball was snapped. The quarterback handed off to a halfback, who pitched it to a wide receiver, who handed off to another player, who handed off again, and again, and again. The ball was handed off fifteen times as players ran all over the field in desperate confusion for several minutes. Finally, the last player with the ball eluded several tacklers and lunged into the end zone for the winning touchdown. I watched this play on YouTube with a friend of mine; he said sarcastically, "That play went just the way the coaches drew it up." In the same way, it's fair to ask, "How often do people make decisions just the way Ignatius drew it up?"

In my experience, not very often. I've never made a decision through the careful step-by-step discernment process outlined in the Spiritual Exercises. I know people who have, but I know many more who have made good decisions based on solid spiritual principles that don't fit neatly into Ignatius's categories. Most decisions are made with the clock ticking, with partial information, and without the time or the means to fully discern the spirits and obtain the kind of confirmation that assures us that the decision is the right one.

Fortunately, we can make good use of Ignatius's principles anyway. Seek God first, know what you truly desire, pay attention to your feelings—these are solid principles that can help you make decisions in any circumstance. *Seek God first*: the choice you're making is not an end in itself but a means to grow closer to God. *Know what you really want*: free yourself of the influence of superficial desires and attachments. *Pay attention to your feelings*: you can usually find the good spirit's leading in the ebb and flow of your emotions.

Also, you get better at discernment and decision making as time goes on. Not long ago I considered taking on a commitment that would have lasted a couple of years and required a lot of work. I had the usual mix of feelings about it that you'd expect, but I didn't do any special discernment. Finally, I sat down with my wife to talk about it, and it very quickly became clear that I shouldn't do it. The price in time and effort was too high; the reasons for doing it had more to do with pride than anything else. I could have made this decision after a lengthy discernment, in one of the ways that Ignatius drew up—but I didn't need to. I had taken some of Ignatius's principles to heart and applied them to the problem.

"Whatever works" is practically an Ignatian motto. Ignatius valued flexibility very highly (as long as the context was solid and known). He had to be flexible in his own life, and he expected people to emerge from the Exercises with an ability to adapt to whatever problems and challenges came their way. He had a relaxed attitude toward rules and systems because he knew that God could be found in all things.

Chapter 12

"Take This Soul and Make It Sing"

Finding God in All Things

One afternoon, long after I finished the Spiritual Exercises, I was working out on the elliptical machine at the gym when one of my favorite songs, "Yahweh," by the Irish rock band U2, popped up on my iPod workout playlist. This song is a prayer. The singer begs God to take the meager things he has and transform them: take this shirt and make it clean; take these hands and do your work with them; take this mouth and give it a kiss; "take this soul and make it sing." I've heard the song dozens of times, but this time it took me to a place I haven't visited very often. A tremendous feeling of gratitude surged up inside me. I felt as if I had actually given some of myself to God, as the song said, partially and fitfully, and that God had received it. I felt both very great and very small—great because God had taken what I have and put it to good use, and small because I was a tiny part of a vast interconnected web of love and grace that filled the visible world and also stretched beyond it.

I stayed in this state for some minutes. While U2 was singing in my headphones, I was sweating and straining to keep up a good pace on the elliptical machine; CNN and ESPN were flickering on the TV monitors in front of me; and dozens of people nearby were stretching, lifting weights, running on treadmills, and riding stationary bikes. It was a strange setting for a transcendent moment. You'd expect it to happen while walking in the silent woods or watching the sun rise over the ocean. Ignatius had his most important vision sitting beside a river. He had another one in a church. Mine came during a cardio workout in the YMCA gym. Later I realized that this was a big part of what God showed me in that experience. God is great, and God is *here*. God can find you at any time. You can find God everywhere. As the Ignatian motto has it, we can find God in all things.

"Something altogether new"

Joy and generosity and the grace to find God in all things are found in a wonderful meditation, the Contemplation to Attain the Love of God, which ends the Spiritual Exercises. Before I go there, though, I want to say something about the third and fourth weeks of the Exercises—the parts of the Exercises that precede the Contemplation.

The second week of the Exercises consists mostly of contemplation of the life of Jesus. The third and fourth weeks are about his passion, death, and resurrection—the great paschal mystery. The goal is to simply be with Jesus. The third week is about Christ's passion, and the grace of the week is the grace of compassion—literally "suffering with." During the fourth week, we are with the resurrected Jesus—specifically the risen Christ present here and now. Joy is the grace of the fourth week.

Joy reaches a crescendo in the Contemplation to Attain the Love of God. It's both mystical and practical, something for your prayer and for your work, food for the spirit and a guide for daily living. It depicts God as Love itself, ceaselessly laboring in this world, infinitely generous. *Attain* means to reach a desired end. The Contemplation is the end we've been headed for ever since the Exercises began.

This vision might well be the product of an actual vision that Ignatius experienced in 1522 while sitting on the banks of the Cardoner River in the town of Manresa in northeastern Spain. He didn't say much about the content of the vision, only that in it he "saw and understood many things" and that he saw familiar things in a new light, as "something altogether new." It wasn't a vision in the literal sense—something seen with the eyes. Rather, Ignatius's mind was opened; it involved his understanding. That's how I understand the Contemplation—as a peek into great mysteries, as revelation of God's nature and personality that we can't know unless God tells us.

"Take, Lord, and receive"

Before giving us the Contemplation, Ignatius makes a couple of observations about how love should be expressed. The first is "love ought to manifest itself in deeds rather than in words." There's a touch of hyperbole there; words have a place in every loving relationship. But deeds have primacy. When we're talking about love, we're talking primarily about deeds of love.

Ignatius's second observation is "love consists in a mutual sharing of goods." Lovers give and receive; these are the deeds Ignatius is talking about. God shares plenty with us.

The question naturally arises, "What do I have to share with God?" In the first point of the Contemplation, Ignatius suggests an answer. Here is one of the great moments of the Spiritual Exercises. The answer is the prayer known as the *Suscipe*, the Latin word for "receive":

> Take, Lord, and receive all my liberty, my memory, my understanding, and all my will—all that I have and possess. You, Lord, have given all that to me. I now give it back to you, O Lord. All of it is yours. Dispose of it according to your will. Give me love of yourself along with your grace, for that is enough for me.

Our response to God's generosity is to give him the only things God doesn't already have: our freedom, our will, our memories, our entire selves. God has given us these things, and he has told us we're free to do whatever we want with them, no strings attached. Now, because we love God and he loves us, we freely give our entire selves back to him. The Suscipe is a prayer of total self-offering. This is the prayer I heard in the words of U2's "Yahweh" as I was working out on the elliptical machine. Take these hands, take this mouth, take this soul—"Take, Lord, and receive."

"His Divine Majesty is truly in all things"

The Contemplation continues:

> This is to reflect how God dwells in creatures: in the elements giving them existence, in the plants giving them life, in the animals conferring upon them sensation, in man bestowing understanding. So He dwells in me and gives me being, life, sensation, intelligence; and makes a temple of me, since I am created in the likeness and image of the Divine Majesty.

If you're looking for the beating heart of Ignatian spirituality, here it is: "God dwells in creatures," and *creatures* has the broadest possible definition. Ignatius said that his fellow Jesuits "should practice the seeking of God's presence in all things—in their conversations, their walks, in all that they see, taste, hear, understand, in all their actions, since His Divine Majesty is truly in all things." The Jesuit theologian St. Robert Bellarmine went even further: "What various powers lie hidden in plants! What strange powers are found in stones," he said.

Some Christian traditions emphasize God's absence from the world. Ignatian spirituality emphasizes God's presence. This flows from a Catholic sacramental perspective that sees God as present in the world through the incarnation of

Christ. It brings God down to earth. "Christ is found in ten thousand places," said the Jesuit poet Gerard Manley Hopkins. It also elevates earth to God; Hopkins also wrote that "the world is charged with the grandeur of God." "Nothing human is merely human," wrote the theologian Ronald Modras. "No common labor is merely common. Classrooms, hospitals, and artists' studios are sacred spaces. No secular pursuit of science is merely secular." Everything that deepens our humanity deepens our knowledge of God.

This expansive view of God's presence should make us humble. Finding God in all things means that no doctrine, religious tradition, philosophical scheme, or devotional practice can exhaust the mystery that is God. We will never reach the end of "all things." We can't grasp the immensity of the cosmos or the vastness of human experience. Something will always lie outside our understanding. Something will always come along to make God present to us in a new way.

Is God present in *all* things? Mathematicians and philosophers talk about a "limit case"—the point at which a system breaks down, the point at which we've taken an idea as far as it can go. Is there a limit case for finding God, a point beyond which God can't be found? I once read an angry comment to a blog post about finding God in all things: "Tell that to the refugee mother in Africa trying to keep her kids from starving." But Christians say that God can be found even in the extreme circumstances of human suffering. Wherever we go, even in the darkest places, Christ is there, too. In fact, he's gone there before us.

By all accounts, Ignatius was a man who found God in all things. One of his close companions wrote, "We frequently saw him taking the occasion of little things to lift his mind to God. From seeing a plant, foliage, a leaf, a flower, any kind of fruit; from the consideration of a little worm or any other animal, he raised himself above the heavens and penetrated the deepest thoughts, and from each little thing he drew doctrine and the most profitable counsels for the spiritual life."

"One who labors"

The Contemplation continues:

> Consider how God works and labors for me in all creatures upon the face of the earth, that is, He conducts Himself as one who labors. Thus, in the heavens, the elements, the plants, the fruits, the cattle etc., He gives being, conserves them, confers life and sensation.

There are many ways to think about God: the king who reigns, the judge, the merciful Lord who forgives sins, the gift giver, the unfathomable Other. Here we're to think of God as "one who labors." God is the worker—the creative power sustaining, healing, and perfecting the world. In the Ignatian view, something is always happening. If God is working, we need to be working, too. We're back to the questions we asked early in the Exercises: "What have I done for Christ? What am I doing for Christ? What ought I to do for Christ?" Christ gave us a task to carry out, not merely a list of truths to affirm.

Cosmologists tell us that everything began in a moment they call the big bang. Before that moment, nothing existed—not even time. Then, in a flash, there was something. Creation is portrayed differently in the book of Genesis, which of course is not history or cosmology. The God of Genesis creates out of chaos, not out of nothing. Before he set to work, "the earth was a formless void and darkness covered the face of the deep." Out of this unpromising raw material came the sun, the moon, and the stars; day and night; the land teeming with plants and animals; and eventually us. This is Ignatius's God—a God who never stops creating. Our world is a kind of chaos—a seething mass of passion, energy, conflict, and desire. The Holy Spirit of God moves through all this, giving us culture, religion, art, science, and all the other elements of our familiar world.

We have a role to play in this creative work. The Holy Spirit is always moving in us to create something beautiful and useful out of raw material that is not very impressive. Christ beckons us to join him in his labors. We work together. That's how we get to know him and to be like him.

All Is Grace

The Spiritual Exercises come to an end with a vision of God as the infinitely generous, inexhaustible giver of gifts:

> To see how all that is good and every gift descends from on high. Thus, my limited power descends from the supreme and infinite power above—and similarly with justice, goodness, pity, mercy, etc.—as rays descend from the sun and waters from a fountain. Then to finish by reflecting within myself. (Ivens)

God dwells in all things; God works in all things; God makes us a gift of all things. God is like the sun, and his gifts are like the sunshine. The sun *is* sunshine. God *is* gift, and the sun always shines.

"What does it matter, all is grace" are the dying words of the lonely, forgotten, anonymous priest in the novel *The Diary of a Country Priest.* They echo the last words of St. Thérèse of Lisieux: "Grace is everywhere." The Spiritual Exercises end on this note—with a numinous vision of light and water, with all as grace, with gifts coming to us endlessly from God, who is Love itself.

There's one more thing. The actual last words of the Contemplation are "finish by reflecting within myself." Ignatius, the ever-practical mystic, asks us to look inside. What does this mean for you? What, if anything, are you going to do about this God who knows you so well and has given you so much? The answer is uniquely yours. Ignatius would be the last person to claim that *he* would know what the answer is. But if you have made the Spiritual Exercises, you should be in a good position to answer that question well. You should at least be in a better position than you used to be, freer than you were, more aware of what you really want, more confident about what's to come, secure in the knowledge that God has found you.

Epilogue

Limping to the Finish Line

In the 1992 Barcelona Olympics, the sprinter Derek Redmond pulled a hamstring muscle halfway through the four-hundred-meter race and collapsed in a heap on the track. In agony, he struggled to his feet and hobbled forward, trying to at least finish a race he'd hoped to win. Suddenly, his father ran onto the track, put his arms around his son, and helped him finish. Hundreds of millions of people watched this touching scene on television. It was an indelible image of what "limping to the finish line" looks like.

I felt a little like Derek Redmond as I limped to the end of the Spiritual Exercises. I had gotten very busy with work, travel, volunteer commitments, and family demands, and some of these things weren't going so well. My spiritual energy had leaked away like the helium seeping out of a party balloon. I still had a few weeks to go to finish the Spiritual Exercises, but I was ready for it to be over. Dennis, my spiritual director, put his arm around me and helped me to the finish line. One of the classic problems with retreats is reentering the real world after an intense mountaintop experience with God. I didn't have that problem; I had been off the mountain for some time.

And I've stayed there. I'm still the same guy. I still work at a job I love. I still love to watch baseball, eat Italian food, take walks with my wife, and work out in the gym. I still love to visit my four kids, who live in Duluth, Nashville, and New York (my favorite place in the whole world). I still try to quiet the little voice in my head that says that the world revolves around me.

But I'm also different in some ways. Perhaps the most important difference has to do with coming to know Jesus in a personal way. The Exercises are mostly about learning to love and follow Jesus. Most of the exercises in the Spiritual Exercises are passages from the gospels that follow him from his birth, through his public ministry, to his suffering, death, and resurrection. The themes and ideas I've written about in this book—coming to grips with sin, hearing God's call, thinking about poverty and humility, discerning the spirits and all the rest of it—happen within the context of coming to know Jesus better and loving him more deeply.

This has given me a deepened sense of God's presence in my daily life as I experience it and live it. My limping finish to the Spiritual Exercises has underscored the point. "Real life" pushed through the door and shouldered the "retreat" aside. It wasn't the ending I dreamed about, but it suited me just fine.

The Exercises brought about a subtly different way of my being in the world. It's hard to describe; it's an attitude—something like a reflective engagement in life. In Ignatian circles this is called being a contemplative in action. The phrase was coined by a Jesuit named Jerónimo Nadal, one of Ignatius's closest associates, who said of Ignatius, "in all things, actions and conversations he perceived and contemplated the presence of God and had an affection for spiritual things, being contemplative even while in action—a matter which he customarily explained by saying: God must be found in all things."

"Contemplative in action" is a kind of watchfulness, a sensitivity to the spiritual currents while I'm engaged in whatever I'm doing. I certainly don't achieve this balance all the time, but I strive for it, and when I get it I feel the joy of it. When I played baseball as a kid, a couple of times I hit the ball on the "sweet spot" of the bat. I swung the bat effortlessly; I hit the ball "just so"; I barely felt the hit, but I heard it and I felt awe as I watched the ball soar up and up into the blue sky, much farther than it did when I tried to hit it hard.

That reflective engagement is the sweet spot. I never knew it was there until I made the Spiritual Exercises. Now I do, and I also know I can't get it by trying hard. Yes, there's plenty of work for me to do, but I'll get to where I want to go by the grace of God. As Ignatius put it in his letter to a busy man, "Make a competent and sufficient effort, and leave the rest to God."

Further Reading and Notes on Sources

Texts of the Spiritual Exercises

Most of the quotes from *The Spiritual Exercises* in this book are from the translation by Louis Puhl, SJ, published by Loyola Press. Several quotes are from the translation and commentary by Michael Ivens, SJ, *Understanding the Spiritual Exercises*, published by Gracewing. Other English translations have been made by George Gans, SJ, Anthony Mottola, and Elder Mullan, SJ, and are available in many published editions. The Puhl and Mullan translations can also be found online.

David L. Fleming, SJ, has made both a contemporary paraphrase and a literal translation in *Draw Me into Your Friendship*, published by the Institute of Jesuit Sources.

Commentary

Michael Ivens' line-by-line commentary in *Understanding the Spiritual Exercises* (Gracewing) is a very valuable resource. *Choosing Christ in the World* by Joseph A. Tetlow, SJ (Institute for Jesuit Sources) is a handbook for directors of the Exercises containing much useful material for retreatants as well.

Other books that I found especially helpful are *The Ignatian Adventure* by Kevin O'Brien, SJ (Loyola Press); *Finding God in All Things* (Ave Maria Press) and *A Friendship Like No Other* (Loyola Press), by William A. Barry, SJ; *Seek God Everywhere* by Anthony de Mello, SJ (Image); *Making Choices in Christ* by Joseph A. Tetlow, SJ (Loyola Press); and *Spiritual Exercises* by Karl Rahner, SJ (Herder & Herder).

The Life of Ignatius

A good edition of Ignatius's autobiography is *A Pilgrim's Journey: The Autobiography of St. Ignatius of Loyola,* edited by Joseph Tylenda, SJ (Ignatius Press). A good biography is *Ignatius Loyola: A Biography of the Founder of the Jesuits* by Philip Caraman, SJ (HarperCollins).

Other Good Books

On Ignatian Spirituality: *The Jesuit Guide to (Almost) Everything* by James Martin, SJ (HarperOne); *What Is Ignatian Spirituality?* by David L. Fleming, SJ (Loyola Press).

On Ignatian Prayer: *A Simple, Life-Changing Prayer: Discovering the Power of St. Ignatius Loyola's Examen* by Jim Manney (Loyola Press); *Inner Compass* by Margaret Silf (Loyola Press); *Contemplatives in Action* by William Barry, SJ, and Robert Doherty, SJ (Paulist).

Online Resources

A wealth of material on the Exercises, discernment, decision making, Ignatian prayer, and other topics can be found online at IgnatianSpirituality.com and OnlineMinistries.creighton.edu.

To Make the Exercises

I recommend making the Spiritual Exercises with the help of a spiritual director if at all possible. A "retreat in daily life," sometimes called a "nineteenth annotation" retreat, does not require time away at a retreat house and usually takes six or seven months. The Exercises can also be experienced in retreats of varying lengths. Contact a local Jesuit retreat center for assistance. See the retreat section of IgnatianSpirituality.com for a directory.

For a self-guided retreat, consider *The Ignatian Adventure* by Kevin O'Brien, SJ (Loyola Press). O'Brien's book is the basis for an online retreat "An Ignatian Prayer Adventure," at IgnatianSpirituality.com. Another self-directed retreat based on the Exercises is *Retreat in the Real World* by Larry Gillick, SJ, et al (Loyola Press). It is also published online at OnlineMinistries.creighton.edu.

Additional Notes on Sources

Chapter 1

Page 8: "A ragged figure flitting from tree to tree at the back of his mind," Flannery O'Connor, *Wise Blood.*

Chapter 2

Page 18: References to *The Spiritual Exercises* here and elsewhere in the chapter are taken from the Michael Ivens translation in *Understanding the Spiritual Exercises.*

Chapter 3

Page 27: Ignatius and the Dominicans at Salamanca, from Philip Caraman, *Ignatius Loyola: A Biography of the Founder of the Jesuits* (Harper & Row).

Page 31: "God desires humans into existence for the sake of friendship": William A. Barry, SJ, *A Friendship Like No Other* (Loyola Press).

Page 32: Material on the examen adapted from Jim Manney, *A Simple, Life-Changing Prayer: Discovering the Power of Ignatius Loyola's Examen* (Loyola Press).

Chapter 4

Page 47: "To lift up the hands in prayer gives God glory," Gerard Manley Hopkins, *Selected Prose,* Gerald Roberts, ed. (Oxford).

Chapter 5

Page 52: *Macbeth*, Act V, v: 24–28.

Page 60: Ignatius on ingratitude, cited in *The Examen Prayer*, Timothy Gallagher (Crossroad).

Chapter 6

Page 67: The "Benedict option" has been popularized by Rod Dreher in his blogging and his book *Crunchy Cons* (Three Rivers Press).

Page 69: *Henry V*, "St. Crispin's Day Speech," http://youtu.be/dDZVxbrW7Ow.

Page 75: On Christian failure, from *Saints and Sanctity*, Walter Burghardt, SJ (Prentice Hall); cited in *The Jesuit Guide to (Almost) Everything* by James Martin, SJ (HarperOne).

Page 76: "Make a competent and sufficient effort," Ignatius's letter to Jerome Vines, in *Letters of St. Ignatius of Loyola*, edited by William J. Young, SJ (Loyola Press).

Chapter 7

Page 80: Bob Dylan, "Gotta Serve Somebody," http://www.youtube.com/watch?v=F2h94gdk_zk.

Page 86: St. Basil on stealing from the poor, cited by Ross Douthat in *Bad Religion* (Free Press).

Chapter 9

Page 105: *A League of Their Own*, "The Hard is What Makes It Great," http://youtu.be/ndL7y0MIRE4.

Chapter 10

Page 123: Ignatius's two sets of rules for discernment are found in sections 313–336 of *The Spiritual Exercises.*

Chapter 11

Page 141: The story of Ignatius opposing Pope Julius III is from Michael Ivens, *Understanding the Spiritual Exercises.*

Page 150: Crazy football play, "Trinity University 28–Millsaps College 24" http://youtu.be/z7oF4ZDigjM.

Chapter 12

Page 153: "Yahweh," U2 live from Chicago, http://youtu.be/GkEQS5SJZPU.

Page 158: Ignatius on seeking God's presence in all things, from *Letters of St. Ignatius of Loyola*, edited by William J. Young, SJ (Loyola Press).

Page 158: "What various powers lie hidden in plants," Robert Bellarmine, SJ, *Spiritual Writings: Classics of Western Spirituality* (Paulist Press).

Page 159: "Nothing human is merely human," Ronald Modras, *Ignatian Humanism: A Dynamic Spirituality for the Twenty-First Century* (Loyola Press).

Page 160: Ignatius finding God in little things, Pedro Ribadaneira, SJ, cited in Joseph Conwell, *Contemplation in Action* (Spokane, WA., Gonzaga University, 1957).

Epilogue

Page 165: "Derek Redmond 1992 Olympics," http://youtu.be/V4S3q6v8nBI.

Acknowledgments

Grateful thanks to

. . . the many friends and mentors who taught me about prayer, especially Bert Ghezzi; Jim Balmer; George Aschenbrenner, SJ; Daniel Schneider, MM; and Dennis Dillon, SJ;

. . . my friends, colleagues, and readers, for their help and encouragement, especially William Barry, SJ; Paul Campbell, SJ; Steve Connor; Joe Durepos; Howard Gray, SJ; Ben Hawley, SJ; Terry Locke; Tom McGrath; Kevin O'Brien, SJ; and Vinita Wright;

. . . to my wife Susan, my best and closest reader.

About the Author

Jim Manney is a popular writer on Ignatian topics (*What's Your Decision?*, *A Simple, Life-Changing Prayer*) as well as the editor of many books on Ignatian spirituality, including *What Is Ignatian Spirituality*. He is senior editor at Loyola Press and lives in Ann Arbor, Michigan.

Continue the Conversation

If you enjoyed this book, then connect with Loyola Press to continue the conversation, engage with other readers, and find out about new and upcoming books from your favorite spiritual writers.

Visit us at **www.LoyolaPress.com** to create an account and register for our newsletters.

Or you can just click on the code to the right with your smartphone to sign up.

Connect with us on the following:

Facebook
facebook.com/loyolapress

Twitter
twitter.com/loyolapress

You Tube
youtube.com/loyolapress

Continue your Ignatian spirituality journey online ...

www.ignatianspirituality.com

Visit us online to

- Join our *E-Magis* newsletter
- Pray the Daily Examen
- Make an online retreat with the *Ignatian Prayer Adventure*
- Participate in the conversation with the dotMagis blog and at facebook.com/ignatianspirituality

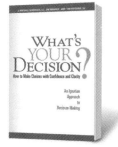

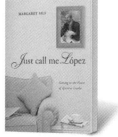